SOTHEBY'S – *Art At Auction*
The Year in Review 1995-96

First published in 1996 by
CONRAN OCTOPUS LIMITED
37 Shelton Street
London WC2H 9HN

British Library Cataloguing in Publication
Data. A catalogue record for this book is
available from the British Library.

ISBN 1 85029 787 8

Commissioning Editor: Denny Hemming
Project Editor: Phyllis Richardson
Desk Editor: Melissa Larner
Production Controller: Julia Golding
Picture Researcher: Jo Alexander

Art Editor: Pep Sala
Designed by Pep Sala –
Communication & Design Services
Printed in Germany by Mohndruck

Endpapers: A pen-and-ink drawing
by Jacqueline Kennedy Onassis, with the
initials J.K. on the base, that was used
on the commemorative book plate for
the sale of Property from the Estate of
Jacqueline Kennedy Onassis.

Page 4: 15th, 16th and 17th century
polychrome wood religious figures from 4
July sale of European Sculpture and Works
of Art, London

SOTHEBY'S
Art at Auction

The Year in Review 1995–96

CONTENTS

As the pages of this book illustrate vividly, 1995–96 was an historic season at Sotheby's. The year's successes included a number of major single-owner collection sales – notably the Joseph H. Hazen Collection of Impressionist and Modern Paintings in New York and the Fattorini Collection of Old Master Paintings in London – but the unquestionable highlights of the season were the sales of the Grand Ducal Collections of the House of Baden in Germany and the Estate of Jacqueline Kennedy Onassis in New York. Though very different in style and content, each of these events stirred the attention of the public in ways seldom seen in the art world.

Apart from impressive sale totals, the two auctions yielded extraordinary numbers and records. Some fifty thousand visitors attended the four days of viewing at Neues Schloss in Baden-Baden, where an enormous exhibition area covered seven thousand square metres. At the Onassis sale, 115,000 copies of the catalogue were sold and 125,000 absentee bids were left, 90,000 of which came from first-time auction participants. Perhaps the most intriguing statistics of all, however, revealed that the vast majority of the buyers at the Baden and Onassis sales were, respectively, German and American, buyers eagerly competing for works of art that represented, in profound and sentimental ways, the history and culture of their own countries.

In addition to separate articles on these landmark sales, this volume also provides two extensive overviews of the season written by George Plumptre in London and Ronald Varney in New York and reviewing Sotheby's diverse sales and special exhibitions. Theme sales have become highly popular, and among this year's outstanding examples was the Irish Sale in London, featuring exceptional paintings, furniture and silver. In addition, a week-long event in New York entitled 'In Celebration of the English Country House' offered a wide array of fine and decorative art, including a masterpiece by John Frederick Herring, Snr, seen opposite (see also p. 56). Two further articles cover Sotheby's involvement in other vital markets. In one, Michel Strauss surveys the dramatic developments in the field of Impressionist and Modern Art over the past fifty years, thirty-five of which he has viewed firsthand as a Sotheby's specialist. In another, David Bennett relates some of the more glamorous sales of jewellery that he has organized since joining the firm over twenty years ago.

The 1995–96 season was also distinguished by a number of key appointments at Sotheby's. The Marquess of Hartington, the son and heir of the Duke of Devonshire and a noted collector of English contemporary art, was appointed Deputy-Chairman of Sotheby's Holdings Board, where he will help chart Sotheby's worldwide growth. And Alice Lam, following a long career as Managing Director of the Hang Seng Bank in Hong Kong, was named Co-Chairman of Sotheby's Asia. With the return of Hong Kong to China in 1997, Mrs Lam will play a central role in expanding Sotheby's presence in Asia.

In this year's edition of *Art at Auction* we have tried to emphasize, in a more visual fashion, the sheer beauty and diversity of the many works of art offered in our salerooms throughout the world. The message these pictures seem to convey more than any other is that very good property is coming on the market and the demand for it is strong.

We hope you will enjoy revisiting with us in these colourful pages a season that was both memorable and historic.

SOTHEBY'S
in Review

The Sotheby's Season 1995–96

THE YEAR IN EUROPE

George Plumptre

THE 1995-96 SEASON brought spectacular sale highlights for Sotheby's in London and Europe, amongst wider activity that confirmed an impressive breadth of operation. From August 1995 to August 1996, Sotheby's held 373 auctions in Europe – just over one a day – 205 of which took place in London at the New Bond Street headquarters. Others were held in Sussex, Scotland, Monaco, Geneva, Zürich, Amsterdam, Milan, Madrid and Stockholm. In addition, Sotheby's mounted in their Bond Street galleries the international company's most ambitious exhibition for nearly a decade, *The Artist and the Country House*, which was greeted with enormous critical and public acclaim.

The year's results demonstrated that against a backdrop of restored confidence and market activity it was once again possible to achieve success in some areas with high volume sales. More particularly, works of the finest quality stimulated the kind of excitement and high prices that had not been seen for more than five years.

During the year Sotheby's achieved world record prices for a remarkable range of items, some of the most distinguished of which included an embroidered sampler from the Tristram Jellinek collection (£27,600); the handwritten manuscript of Paul McCartney's lyric for *Getting Better* (£161,000); the Sandwich royal ship model (£287,500, see p.247); and a life-size Indian portrait of the Emperor Jahangir (£573,500). Similar records for individual artists included Orazio Gentileschi (£5,061,500); J. B. Yeats (£804,500); and L. S. Lowry (£282,000, see p.62).

Amongst these individual successes, one event stands out like a colossus – the sale of 25,000 objects from the Grand Ducal Collections of Baden in Germany (see pp 25–7). In addition, some of the most spectacular prices were achieved by jewellery and gem stones.

Sotheby's has established an unrivalled reputation for conducting country house auctions. The atmosphere engendered by a sale 'on site' is something that cannot be recreated in the saleroom. Baden-Baden was a country house auction of unparalled proportions, but other landmark events during the year included the first ever house sale in Denmark, at Aalholm Slot, and the sale at Ickworth, in Suffolk. The four-day auction at Aalholm nearly doubled the pre-sale estimate to reach a total for some 1,800 lots of over £2 million. Perhaps the most significant aspect of this sale was the fact that the majority of the buyers, among a truly international audience, were Danish, and as a result many of the objects of national importance remained in the country.

At Ickworth (see p.249), a property bought by the National Trust in 1956, Sotheby's were instructed by the Marquess of Bristol, whose family have lived there since the eighteenth

Opposite: *Particularly notable in July's sale of Old Master Drawings were works from the collection at Corsham Court, including Agnolo Bronzino's* The Meeting of Joseph and Jacob in Egypt, *sold for £293,000.*

Right: *This life-size Indian portrait of* The Emperor Jahangir Holding a Globe, *dated 1617, broke world records when it sold in October for £573,500.*

century, to sell the contents of the private apartments. The two-day sale attracted enormous interest and the final total achieved was well in excess of £2 million. The lots included a number of outstanding and historic paintings, items of furniture and works of art commissioned or collected by members of the Hervey family (Earls and then Marquesses of Bristol) during more than two centuries. Two paintings in particular, both attributed to Sir Anthony van Dyck, exemplified the kind of sensation that can be produced at a country house sale. The first, a self portrait of the artist with a sunflower, escalated from its pre-sale estimate of £15,000-20,000 to reach £210,500, and the second, a portrait said to be of the Marchesa Balbi, sold for £133,500 on a pre-sale estimate of £4,000-6,000.

In the saleroom, paintings of undisputed quality and distinguished provenance, particularly in the Impressionist and Old Master categories, produced results that had not been seen for many years. The late November auction of Impressionist and Modern Art was anticipated with great interest and was notable for the sale of Gauguin's *Femmes au bord de la rivière* (see p.76), which achieved a price of £3,191,500. A few days later, the sale of Old Master Paintings presented a catalogue of works of great distinction, primarily from two private collections – the Bentinck-Thyssen Collection, and the Castle Howard Collection. The fifty-five lots of Bentinck-Thyssen paintings encapsulated the best of twentieth-century connoisseurship with works by Dutch, Italian and French artists. Most celebrated was Rembrandt's *Cupid Blowing a Soap Bubble* (see p.48), which sold for £3,851,500. Gentileschi's *The Finding of Moses* had hung at Castle Howard since 1798, when it was purchased from the Orléans Collection by the 5th Earl of Carlisle. A truly magnificent painting, it commanded a rare presence when displayed in Sotheby's Bond Street gallery. The sale

These flamboyant costumes for Diaghilev and the Ballets Russes from the Castle Howard Collection were sold during 'Russian Week' at Sotheby's. They fetched, from left to right, £18,400; £5,750 and £4,370.

achieved a total of over £20 million, the highest for any London auction of Old Master Paintings for nearly five years.

Only days after these memorable events, Sotheby's Bond Street galleries were transformed into quite a different mood for 'Russian Week', an event whose style was again matched by saleroom succccess. Few visitors will forget being greeted at the door by Sotheby's usually sombre-uniformed commissionaire Andrew Deacon attired as a Cossack. The Castle Howard Collection produced perhaps the most flamboyant element – sumptuous costumes for Diaghilev's Ballets Russes. These, together with the rich mix of Russian paintings, icons, porcelain and other works of art, and a final sale total of over £5 million, highlighted the importance of Russia's artistic heritage.

January is traditionally a quiet month in the London auction calendar, but in 1996 Sotheby's mounted a three-week exhibition, *The Artist and the Country House*. Arising from a desire to revive what in the past had been a strong Sotheby's tradition of mounting major exhibitions, the galleries showed a total of 144 views of British houses, all from private collections and many previously unseen in public, dating from the fifteenth century to the present day. Ten thousand visitors attended, including HRH The Prince of Wales. A separate reception was held for the Prince's Institute of Architecture. All were captivated by the unique display of British cultural history, and media acclaim for the exhibition was equally enthusiastic, typified by *The International Herald Tribune*'s comment that this was a 'major artistic event'.

In May 1995 Sotheby's London held their first Irish Sale, offering a wonderful array of Irish paintings and works of art, from furniture to silver, glass and Belleek porcelain, bringing a total of £3.65 million. When the second Irish Sale was held in May 1996 all previous expectations were exceeded as the total reached £4.24 million. The sale's high points were provided by two works by Jack Butler Yeats. The first, *Leaving the Raft*, set a new world record for the artist of £661,500, which only stood for a few minutes until *A Farewell to Mayo*, previously bought by Sir Laurence Olivier for his wife, Vivien Leigh, sold for £804,500 (see p.98).

Orazio Gentileschi's The Finding of Moses, *painted for Charles I, is probably the greatest Baroque work of art made by an Italian working in England. It sold for £5,061,500, the highest price paid for any work by the artist.*

Shortly afterwards, in June 1996, Sotheby's made a welcome addition to the Bond Street galleries. Situated on the ground floor and open all day, The Café offers a wide selection of refreshments for clients and visitors.

Although Sotheby's will not be able to hold auctions in France until 1998, when new government legislation ends a centuries-old monopoly for French firms, we have held auctions at the glamorous Sporting d'Hiver, in Monte-Carlo, for many years. There, in June 1996, a sumptuous array of eighteenth-century French furniture and works of art, principally from two highly distinguished collections – the Delplace Collection and the Weiller Collection – provided one of the season's outstanding events in an auction that doubled its pre-sale estimate to realize a total in excess of £7 million. From the Weiller Collection a pair of Louis XV commodes in gold and red vernis Martin topped the results and fetched FF8,636,500 (see p.192), while, from the Delplace Collection, a bookcase commode stamped 'J. F. Oeben' was sold for FF7,068,500 (see p.190).

Despite these successes, the climax of the London auction year was reserved for the closing weeks of the summer season and a series of sales in which the quality of works offered was only matched by the drama of events. The auctions included English Furniture, where a selection of eighteenth-century pieces dominated a sale achieving a total of £4.5 million. Amongst a range of items that combined the exemplary craftsmanship of the age with distinguished provenance, undoubtedly the greatest treasure was a pair of mahogany armchairs attributed to one of the master cabinet-makers of the period, William Vile (see p.179). They were made for one of the supreme English collections, which was formed by the Earl of Shaftesbury at his home, St Giles's House, in Dorset, and they doubled their pre-sale estimate to achieve a price of £837,500.

In late June, the evening sale of Impressionist and Modern Art, which included paintings from the Gutzwiller collection, achieved results of over £31 million, the

The British Rail Pension Fund Collection of European Sculpture and Works of Art was auctioned in July for a total of £13,698,180, constituting a world record for any auction of works of art. The highest price was achieved by this Romanesque gilt-bronze candlestick base which sold for £4,401,500.

highest total for any sale of Impressionist and Modern Art since 1990. Seven paintings that each fetched more than £1 million included a work of major importance by Cézanne, *Grands arbres au jas de bouffan*, which sold for £5,171,500 (see pp.76–77). The sale was distinguished by very strong bidding from private collectors.

Two days later it was the Contemporary Art department whose sale produced the best results since 1990, with a total of £7,353,750. The most valuable work sold was Dubuffet's *Hommes et arbres somnambuliques*, which went over its high estimate to reach £826,500.

Many people eagerly awaited the summer sale of Old Master paintings containing a small but superlative group of Dutch paintings from the Fattorini Collection, which was brought together during the 1940s by Enrico Fattorini. A Yorkshireman of Italian extraction, he came from a family who established themselves as successful merchants in Bradford during the mid-nineteenth century. His discerning eye and taste for Dutch paintings made him one of the most significant collectors of these pictures during the middle of this century. Eight paintings sold for a total of £5,666,000, with the three outstanding works each fetching over £1 million. Pieter de Hooch's *A Maid with a Broom and a Pail in a Sunlit Courtyard* (see pp.48–49) sold for £2,201,500; William van der Velde the Younger's *A Calm* (see pp.50–51) sold for £1,376,500, and Paulus Potter's *Two Cows and a Bull in a Meadow* sold for £1,079,500. The sale's highest price, however, was achieved by the outstanding work in the group of paintings that came from the British Rail Pension Fund, whose Old Master Collection has made such a distinguished contribution to Sotheby's sales in recent years. Goya's *The Death of a Picador* (see pp.44–45) sold for £2,586,500 and the collection overall achieved a total in excess of £5.5 million out of the sale total of over £16 million. Such high quality paintings were complemented by the sale of Old Master drawings that followed the same day. Particularly notable were the drawings from Corsham Court, one of England's most distinguished surviving collections. In a sale totalling over £2 million, Bronzino's magnificent drawing, *The Meeting of Joseph and Jacob in Egypt,* sold for £293,000.

On the following day, the British Rail Pension Fund Collection attracted highly competitive bidding and exceptional prices. Their collection of European Sculpture and Works of Art has been renowned for the superb quality and the rarity of many of its pieces. At the end of the sale of ninety-two lots, the total achieved was £13,698,180, a sum that constituted a world record for any auction of works of art and exceeded those of three of Sotheby's previously most historic sales: the von Hirsch Collection (1979), the Mentmore House Sale (1978) and the Ducal Collections of the House of Baden (1995). The highest price was achieved by a Romanesque gilt-bronze candlestick base, which was sold for £4,401,500. However, most of the attention was fixed on a gilt copper and cloisonné enamel reliquary *chasse*, commemorating the martyrdom, burial and ascent of the soul of St Thomas à Becket, made in Limoges *circa* 1165. It eventually sold for £4,181,500 to an anonymous private collector, amidst widespread discussion and suggestions that it should be purchased for the nation. However, the national institutions were outbid, as the sale price exceeded their limit. Yet, one week later, it was revealed that the successful purchaser, Lord Thomson, had decided with great magnanimity to withdraw his bid. This action enabled the Becket *chasse* to be acquired jointly by the National Heritage Memorial Fund and the Victoria and Albert Museum in London.

Sotheby's integral role in the events leading up to and following the sale of the Becket *chasse* is tied to their longstanding involvement with the collection of the British Rail Pension fund, a relationship that has continued for more than twenty years. This kind of commitment confirms the company's position as the world's leading auction house, and a repository of scholarly, aesthetic and professional expertise. In the public spotlight of auctions, behind the scenes in the offices of expert departments, and in the ever-changing face of the galleries, the combined range of skills is formidable. Such a sale, linked as it is to a distinguished auctioning heritage, confirms that Sotheby's great tradition will continue into the future.

A gilt-copper and cloisonné enamel reliquary chasse *commemorating the martyrdom, burial and ascent of the soul of St Thomas à Becket sold for £4,181,500 in the July sale of the British Rail Pension Fund Collection in London.*

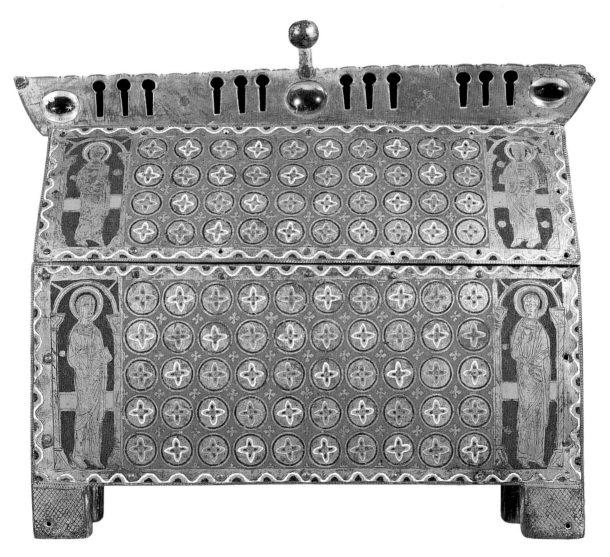

THE YEAR IN NEW YORK

Ronald Varney

WHILE THE TWIN PEAKS OF THE 1995–96 auction season in New York were doubtless the autumn sale of the Joseph H. Hazen Collection, a classic group of Impressionist and Modern pictures that yielded superb prices, and the spring auction of the Jacqueline Kennedy Onassis estate, a dream-like event that cast its spell far and wide, the season itself was a play of many thrilling scenes and dramatic twists. Indeed, the towering pictorial auction banners that appeared in the great windows fronting York Avenue seemed appropriate heralds for a season of high theatre in the saleroom.

In a serendipitous act of scheduling, the early fall season offered the collections of three of the most celebrated designers and taste-makers in America – Dorothy 'Sister' Parish, Ralph Lauren and Robert Metzger. Each sale was an occasion for high-style exhibition design, the Sotheby's galleries evoking, in lavish room-like settings, the individual flair and signature of each personality. A fine array of American, English and Continental furniture, decorations, paintings, rugs and silver had graced Mrs Parrish's elegant Fifth Avenue maisonette, a place that magically came to life in the public exhibition. Amid a saleroom packed with collectors, decorators and enthusiasts all competing vigorously for a piece of this charming collection, the sale brought $1,364,516, well above the estimate of $937,550.

This kind of success was repeated in October with the sale of the Ralph Lauren Collection, which consisted of a large group of fine English and Continental furniture and decorations that were once showcased in Mr Lauren's home and among the fashion

The October 1995 sale of The Ralph Lauren Collection began two weeks of 'Great Designers at Sotheby's'. The Lauren collection of English and Continental furniture brought a sale total of $2,512,028.

collections in his stores and showrooms across America. With Sotheby's exhibition rooms done up in classic Ralph Lauren style, the collection stirred great excitement and brought $2,512,028. Two weeks later these 'Great Designers at Sotheby's' sales concluded with the auction of the Robert Metzger Collection. This large and eclectic group of furniture, candlesticks, mirrors, chairs, clocks and screens – including a most remarkable ensemble of shagreen decorative items, all of which sold for multiples of the estimate – comprised a wonderful autobiography, emphasizing Mr Metzger's taste for objects of bold, unusual qualities. The sale, another marathon of intense bidding, brought $1,729,858, with expectations once again exceeded.

'Asian Arts Week' at Sotheby's New York, which occurs twice yearly, offers outstanding examples of works of art, paintings and furniture from India, Southeast Asia, China, Korea and Japan. The highlight of the September sale of Indian and Southeast Asian Art was an important group of sculptures from India, Thailand and Cambodia consigned by the renowned New York gallery owners Mr and Mrs Klaus G. Perls. An impressive total of $2.7 million established a new record in America for a sale in this field. The top lot, from the Perls Collection, was a 'South Indian Bronze figure of Shiva' poised in his cosmic dance within a flaming halo, which sold to a private collector for $151,000 (see p. 145).

The 'Magnificent Jewelry' sale in October featured one of the finest private collections of jewellery ever to be seen at auction. The centrepiece was a 'Fancy Deep Blue Diamond Ring' weighing 6.70 carats. Soaring above its estimate, the ring sold for $3,522,500 and, following a custom in this rarefied field of collecting, its new owner promptly renamed the stone 'The Magnificent Graff Blue Heart'. An even more intriguing piece from this

collection was a spectacular diamond necklace, *circa* 1900, made in part with a fringe of twenty-eight old-mine diamonds from the great *comb à pampilles* of the French Crown Jewels. This wondrous piece, owned previously by the Dowager Viscountess Harcourt, sold for $244,500.

Moving into the high gear of the autumn season, a number of important sales took place in a range of collecting fields, with generally excellent results. The Richard Meech Collection of George I and later silver, comprising many fine examples of the work of Paul de Lamerie and Paul Storr, brought $1,562,470, nicely complementing the earlier auction at Sotheby's New York of Mr Meech's collection of seventeenth-century and Queen Anne silver, which yielded $1.19 million in October 1993. Two days after the Meech sale a set of four George III silver sauce tureens more than doubled its high estimate, bringing $629,500 in a sale of English and Continental silver.

Also repeating earlier successes was a collection of rare illustrated books from the Library of Dr Otto Schäfer, which made a stunning $5,439,222 in November. A German industrialist and bibliophile, Dr Schäfer assembled the most important private collection of books in Europe since World War II. Combined with two previous sales from this monumental collection, the latest auction brought the total for the Schäfer Collection to $17.9 million.

The major paintings sales in November came rapid fire, drawing an enormous number of visitors to the exhibition galleries. The busy proceedings of the November sales were made all the more engaging by the strong results that were achieved in every field. The Nineteenth-Century European Paintings sale on 1 November, for example, saw seven of the top ten lots selling well above their high estimates, with a record price of $3,412,500

This spectacular diamond necklace was previously owned by the Dowager Viscountess Harcourt. Made in part from diamonds from the French Crown Jewels, it sold for $244,500 in the October sale of 'Magnificent Jewelry'.

achieved for Millet's majestic painting *L'été, les glaneuses* (see p.70). The Contemporary Art sale on the evening of 15 November totalled $19.89 million and was one of the strongest in this field in five years, with a record price of $3,962,500 set for Arshile Gorky's masterpiece *Scent of Apricots on the Fields* (see p.88). The Latin American Paintings sale on 21 November was another record breaking affair, with a 1942 expressionistic painting by Mexican artist Roberto Matta, *Disasters of Mysticism*, bringing a record price of £1,652,500.

The build-up to an important Impressionist and Modern art sale is occasioned by considerable suspense, as the art world awaits the results of an event that often defines the character, and success, of an entire auction season. Coming on the heels of the immensely successful spring sale of the Donald and Jean Stralem Collection, the November sale of fifteen paintings from the collection of film producer Joseph H. Hazen, a great figure from the days of the old Hollywood studio system, prompted high expectations. In a breathless bidding war, the centrepiece of the Hazen Collection, van Gogh's lush forest scene *Sous-Bois* (see p.78), painted a month before the artist took his own life, sold for almost $27 million. The Hazen Collection brought $51.8 million, one of the highest single-owner sale totals in auction history.

Superlatives continued to mark the path of the fall season in New York. Also in November, in the first two-day wine sale to be held in New York, Sotheby's, in partnership with the wine merchant Sherry-Lehmann, achieved a total of $2.09 million, the highest ever for a wine auction in America. The Tribal Art sale the same month brought its highest total in five years, with a rare Cook Islands Rarotongan head of a staff god (see p.162), which had been stored in a closet for more than 150 years, selling for a record price of $530,500. And on 8 December, in one of the most successful sales of Antiquities and Islamic Art ever in America, an Assyrian gypsum relief fragment depicting a winged guardian divinity (see p.167) sold for $5,667,500, five times its estimate. Coming from the Collection of Mr and Mrs Klaus G. Perls, which figured prominently in the early successes of the season, this piece served as a fitting endnote to the fall sales.

In the New York art world the month of January is synonymous with Americana. With the 'Winter Antiques Show' drawing huge crowds to the Seventh Regiment Armoury on Park Avenue and the major auctions of the year taking place in the fields of American Furniture and American Folk Art, January has a highly festive air, despite its brittle, gloomy weather. This year's 'Americana Week' at Sotheby's was all the more exciting because of the appearance on the market of one of the truly great collections of Americana, featuring extraordinary examples of seventeenth-century, Queen Anne, Chippendale and Federal furniture. Formed by Mr and Mrs Adolph Henry Meyer of Birmingham, Michigan, this landmark collection drew over seven hundred people.

Lot after lot prompted fierce bidding struggles, and prices rocketed well beyond the estimates: a Federal inlaid sewing table, for example, estimated at $30,000-40,000, went for $189,500; and a Queen Anne chest of drawers, expected to bring $40,000-60,000, sold for $321,500. Anticipation had no doubt been whetted by the appearance months earlier of *Masterpieces of Americana*, a lavishly illustrated volume on the collection, published by Sotheby's Books, which received wide attention. The absolute star of the sale, the Samuel Whitehorn Queen Anne block-and-shell carved mahogany kneehole desk made in Newport, Rhode Island, estimated at $800,000-1,200,000, brought $3,632,500, the second highest price ever paid for a piece of American furniture. At the sale's end, the Meyer Collection totalled $11.18 million, doubling its estimate and leaving an indelible mark on the field of Americana.

Theme sales have become increasingly popular at Sotheby's. This season saw the advent of a weeklong series of auctions entitled 'In Celebration of the English Country House', encompassing paintings, furniture and decorations. The highlight of the week, a sale of English Sporting Paintings, offered one of the finest examples of this genre ever to appear at auction, John Frederick Herring's *The Start of the Epsom Derby*, dated 1835, which more than doubled its estimate in fetching an impressive $2,250,000 (see p.56). The popularity of these sales bodes well for their continuance on the calendar.

Following on in April, the Jacqueline Kennedy Onassis sale (see pp.22–4) held many extraordinary moments and revelations and was unprecedented in auction history.

As if there were not enough atomic charges left in the air by the Onassis sale, no sooner was it over than the spring series of major paintings sales began. The Impressionist sale showed the continuing vitality and confidence of this market, with a group of paintings by Schiele, Chagall and Balthus from the Georg Waechter Memorial Foundation selling for $8.48 million. High points were also reached in American Paintings, when records were established for works by Norman Rockwell and Maxfield Parrish and a startling price of $4,842,500 was paid for Sargent's *Capri Girl*

A set of four George III silver sauce tureens by Benjamin Smith, London, 1807, one of the highlights of the October English and Continental Silver sale.

The Old Master Paintings sale of May 1996 produced record prices. Included was this Piedmontese School painting, Elegant Figures Seated in the Picture and Porcelain Cabinet of a Palace, *which sold for $162,000.*

Opposite: Kandinsky's Das Jungste Gericht, *from the November auction of the Jospeh H. Hazen Collection, which brought $51.8 million, the tenth highest single-owner sale total in auction history.*

(see p.101). Parrish's *Daybreak* (see p.100), the artist's most widely published image, sold for $4,292,500. The spring Old Master Paintings sale featured a work by Pierre-Joseph Redouté, *An Elaborate Still Life of Flowers* (see p.47), that established a world record price for the artist when it sold for $1,487,500, over ten times its high estimate. The Old Master Paintings sales were exceptional throughout the season, with many outstanding works coming fresh to the market from some of the most renowned American and European private collections.

In a season that brought to the market an extraordinary number of works from the Tiffany Studios, the May sale of Tiffany lamps from the Warshawsky Corporate Collection stood out. Proving the unquenchable thirst among collectors for the finest quality Tiffany pieces, the collection totalled an impressive $4,275,297, with many works fetching multiples of their high estimates. A related sale that took place in June featured a small but important group of jewellery and art objects from the Collection of Lillian Nassau, the renowned dealer and collector of Art Nouveau and Art Deco. She was a pioneer in her field, and her collection included rings, purses, hair combs and objects made by the most prominent craftsmen of the twentieth century. Because of the great interest in Art Deco and Art Nouveau in Asia, a selection from the Nassau Collection was exhibited in Tokyo in March.

This sale, and its presentation, in many ways exemplified the best of what Sotheby's has done for over two centuries – to bring passionately gathered artworks to an enthusiastic market.

ICON OF AN ERA
THE ESTATE OF JACQUELINE KENNEDY ONASSIS

John Culme

Forty thousand people attended the four-day exhibition prior to the sale of the Jacqueline Kennedy Onassis Estate. The sale itself, which took place from 23 to 26 April 1996, attracted record numbers.

Opposite: Jacqueline Kennedy during an official visit to India in 1962. On a boat trip to a 17th-century lake palace, the First Lady gazes up at an admiring crowd gathered along the banks.

FROM THE MOMENT Diana D. Brooks brought the gavel down upon the first lot in the sale of the Estate of Jacqueline Kennedy Onassis, it was clear to everyone present that this would indeed be an historic auction. The promise of more than a year of planning and preparation was being realized. Forty thousand people attended the four-day exhibition prior to the sale, demonstrating an unprecedented amount of interest. Certainly, this was no ordinary event. Visitors expressed feelings of personal involvement with the Kennedy history, each supplying similar reasons for attending the event. One woman, whose 'wish list' of bids included a pair of eighteenth-century English enamel candlesticks used at the White House during President and Mrs Kennedy's residence, admitted that she was there because she was a 'child of the 1950s' and had looked up to Jacqueline Kennedy as a role model. As a *New York Times* columnist put it, 'For the public, [Sotheby's] are not selling things. They are selling yesterday, when the world was young.'

Of course, Sotheby's is not unused to celebrity auctions; the company practically invented them. As long ago as the 1850s, the firm offered such personal items as a pair of Queen Victoria's slippers and a complete set of Crimean War views by the Queen's photographer, Roger Fenton. The market in autographed letters and manuscripts is as old as collecting itself, but more recently, especially after the opening of the Collector's Department at Belgravia in the early 1970s, Sotheby's has responded to the cult of personality with ever more sophistication. It seems that trinkets of the nobility and pop star paraphernalia are the contemporary equivalents of medieval relics. To possess them is, for some, a mystical experience. Public demand is there and Sotheby's is the agent. The huge success achieved by the sales of the Duchess of Windsor's jewels (1987) and the collections of Andy Warhol (1988), Elton John (1988) and

Greta Garbo (1990), among others, is proof of the high degree of fascination surrounding these icons. These sales contained the components necessary for a grand event: collectors whose lives have touched or inspired us in some way, and possessions that are intimately connected with those lives. Such ingredients are as irresistible now as they have ever been.

The Jacqueline Kennedy Onassis sale satisfied all these criteria, and it is hardly surprising that bidding became so passionate. There are abundant examples of objects that provoked bidding wars between committed buyers. Among the most astounding of these competitions was that which resulted in the $211,500 paid for Mrs Onassis' triple-strand imitation pearl necklace, estimated to realize between $500 and $700. Jewellery always inspires a certain awe on these occasions; little else apart from the written word can be so evocative. Thanks to a photograph of the First Lady taken at the White House in August 1962, in which she holds her son, John, in her arms while he toys with her pearls, the necklace is now imbued with a distinctive meaning.

Indeed, the entire auction was pervaded by a sense of Jacqueline Kennedy Onassis' style and spirit, a fact often remarked upon by visitors to the exhibition. Some were intrigued by echoes of the young Jacqueline Bouvier's family background, as illustrated by her choice in furniture and furnishings, books and many examples of eighteenth- and early nineteenth-century French fine and decorative art. Others were drawn by such pieces as the Louis XVI ormolu-mounted black and white marble obelisks and the ormolu-mounted mahogany *bureau plat* and *cartonnier*, which was used by President Kennedy for the historic signing of the Nuclear Test Ban Treaty of 1963. Yet others were impressed by her love of Indian art: miniatures from the subcontinent as well as jewellery from, and inspired by, India and Pakistan. Even though, as First Lady, she had

Session Five of the auction contained many pieces of jewellery that the public associate with Mrs Onassis' elegant image, including the simulated pearl necklace (not shown) that sold for $211,500.

President Kennedy, surrounded by members of his cabinet and congressional leaders, signs the Nuclear Test Ban Treaty of 5 August 1963. The bureau plat *and* cartonnier *sold for $1,432,500 (see p.194).*

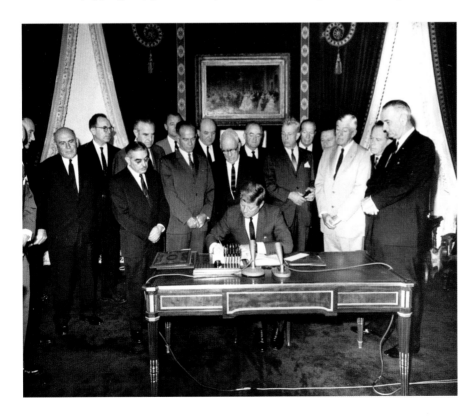

travelled to the countries on goodwill visits in 1962, when she was hailed as the *Ameriki Rani* ('Queen of America'), few had realized how much she had taken the two places to heart. A journalist covering the auction for an Indian newspaper was not alone in her surprise at Mrs Onassis' interest in this area and took particular delight in the Mewar School *Portrait of a Stallion with His Groom* of about 1760.

This miniature may have appealed to Mrs Onassis for its evocation of India, but it must also have spoken to the accomplished horsewoman in her. Many of the lots sold in the auction reflected that side of her, from the four etchings by Stefano Della Bella (1610–64) of *Exotic Figures on Horseback* to John Wootton's portrait, *Lord Bateman's Arabian* of 1733–34. Her love of horses and riding was also apparent from the three leather hunting saddles that were included in the sale.

Apart from the enormous logistical effort that the eight-day exhibition and sale period entailed, the auction produced some truly heroic numbers. Approximately six thousand items were sold during nine sessions encompassing eighteen collecting categories. Twelve thousand attended the sales, and 115,000 copies of the catalogue were sold. Some 125,000 absentee bids were left, and of the 643 buyers, 445 were new to Sotheby's. The auction total of $34,457,470, a striking multiple of the pre-sale estimate of around $5 million, was reached after 99 percent of the lots sold above their high estimates. Perhaps the most remarkable result was achieved in Session Five, which offered 'Fashion Jewelry'. Though estimated to bring $37,000–54,000, the session totalled an astounding $2,456,340, forty-five times the high estimate.

So, it was a combination of factors that made this a particularly memorable auction. Above all, it was the public's response to the memory of a much-loved celebrity that contributed to its success. In her announcement to the press immediately following the last session of the sale, Diana D. Brooks paid tribute to Jacqueline Kennedy Onassis. Visibly moved by the moment and aware that the sale marked another decisive chapter in Sotheby's history, she spoke of Mrs Onassis' 'grace and style, her dignity, her courage', which had underpinned the results of this extraordinary event.

FOUR HUNDRED YEARS OF HISTORY
THE GRAND DUCAL COLLECTIONS OF BADEN

Marcus Linell

THE SALE OF THE Grand Ducal Collections of Baden was the largest fine art auction in living memory. The Margraves of Baden are one of Germany's oldest princely families, with a title that was first adopted in 1112. The acquisition of works of art is an important part of their history, and inventories of their fifteen residencies, dating back to 1666, attest to this.

This auction was not, however, the first of its kind for the Margraves of Baden. The initial recorded sale from the collections took place when a branch of the Baden line ended with the death of Margrave August Georg in 1771. As a result, a large collection of works of art that had belonged to his mother, Sibylla Augusta, was sold at auction in Offenburg in 1775. The next sale occurred in 1808, when Carl Friedrich auctioned off the art collection that had been stored in the Markgräfer Hof, an occasional residence of the Margraves in Basel, in order to satisfy debts incurred with the acquisition of land.

His Royal Highness Max, Margrave of Baden, is currently Head of the House of Baden and related to all the main royal houses of Europe. His mother, Margravine Theodora, Princess of Greece and Denmark, was a sister of the Duke of Edinburgh. In 1966 he married Her Imperial and Royal Highness the Archduchess Valerie of Austria, and they have four children, of whom Prince Bernhard, now aged twenty-five, is heir.

In 1910, at the height of its power, the Grand Duchy of Baden was larger than the state of Connecticut, and had more than twice the population. By 1919, at the end of World War I, the State claimed almost half of this great estate and its works of art. As a result many objects from the fifteen castles, palaces and houses previously owned by the Margraves were transferred for storage to Neues Schloss in Baden-Baden, where they remained, largely unseen, for the last seventy-five years.

In November 1994, the Margrave and his financial advisors, working on a process of restructuring and modernization, invited Sotheby's to Neues Schloss to discuss the possibility of a sale of some of the family's huge collection of furniture and works of art. In 1995 Sotheby's had the privilege of overseeing the third and largest auction of the Margraves' property, and of coming into contact with one of the most important private collections in Germany. It was a task that involved the discovery of unknown objects, as well as detailed research. Most of the pieces in the collection had been in the possession of the Margraves of Baden since they were created, whether in the Middle Ages or in succeeding centuries. Furniture, paintings, ceramics, and precious *objets d'art*, many of them made for the family by the leading artists and craftsmen of the time, filled the 105 rooms.

The excitement for the Sotheby's team of visiting experts was palpable, as they went about the romantic job of exploring rooms that had been unused since 1919, the contents of which were mostly shrouded in dust covers. A cupboard held treasures collected from the seventeenth century. A lavishly embroidered French silk *banjan*, or loose robe, dating from about 1730, appeared in perfect condition. An eighteenth-century tea table made for the Swedish royal family and brought to Baden-

The fifteen-day auction of the Grand Ducal Collections was held in a marquee in the courtyard of Neues Schloss, which overlooks the spa town of Baden-Baden on the edge of the Black Forest.

Most of the items in the sale were made specifically for one of the family residences and have never been owned outside the family.
Above: *Preparations for auction at Neues Schloss.* Below: *A vintage photograph shows the family's Karlsruhe residence decorated for the Christmas holidays.*

Baden in 1810 by Queen Friederike of Sweden, the daughter of the reigning Margrave, was found under a pile of blankets. It was bought for just over a million dollars, the highest price paid for any item in the sale. A large nineteenth-century German chandelier was discovered in the cellar of the castle, wrapped in newspaper dated 1876; it sold for over ten times its estimate.

Even humble objects conveyed a peculiar feeling of intimacy and the uncanny sense that time had stopped in 1919. There was unfinished needlework in sewing boxes, children's toys, still in their original boxes, purses and bags, a pair of embroidered shoes made for the Margrave's golden wedding anniversary in 1905, and many other touching records of an aristocratic Germany that ended with the upheavals of World War I.

The preliminary survey was completed by Christmas of 1994 and established a value of DM80 million, and the Margrave's hope was that the collection would be acquired by the State of Baden-Württemburg. Unfortunately there were insufficient funds to purchase the whole collection. As the politicians deliberated, it became clear that at least a portion of the collection would be sold at auction.

A provisional sale date of June was agreed, and in January 1995 thirty-seven Sotheby's experts visited Neues Schloss to catalogue and calculate estimates of the vast collection, about which, despite its importance, almost nothing had been written. A printed version of the earliest inventory, made in 1666, survived and was an invaluable source of information, as many older pieces still bore their original inventory numbers. Some objects were tagged with several labels relating to later inventories made by the family for one of the Margraves' other estates. A full-time archivist was employed and this research, preserved in the catalogue, helped to establish the precise historical background of many of the major pieces in the collection.

Meanwhile, the State asked for more time to consider their decisions, and the Margrave agreed to postpone the sale until October. This was a costly decision for him, but it was a great help to the State and incidentally allowed Sotheby's experts more time for research.

As the importance of the collection became clearer, and the sale deadline neared, the vari-ous State bodies finally came to an agreement and released funds. A group of rare early Meissen porcelain was bought for Schloss Favorite, the Baroque summer palace built in 1710–11 for the Margravine Sibylla Augusta (1675–1733). Here it would be reunited with the rest of her collection, which had all been acquired directly from the Meissen factory and was second only in importance to the collection of the founder of the factory, Augustus the Strong, Elector of Saxony.

A number of objects were eventually purchased by the State. A spectacular series of tapestries, seven of which were presented to Cardinal de Rohan, Prince-bishop of Strasbourg, by Louis XVI and later acquired by Grand Duke Ludwig of Baden, have returned to Schloss Mannheim. Formerly one of the family's residences, it now houses the University and has State rooms that are open to the public.

Various public collections of Baden-Württemberg were greatly enriched by items from the sale. The Badisches Landesmuseums of Karlsruhe brought out a colour catalogue of the 257 objects it acquired which are now on view to the public. Another catalogue details purchases made by the Stattliche Schlosser und Garten (the equivalent of the National Trust) and returned by them to seven important residences that were once owned by the Margraves of Baden. These houses are now wholly or partly open to the public and the objects will be displayed, in some cases, in the very rooms and situations for which they were originally created.

Four weeks before the sale, the State released funds for the purchase of the highlight of the whole collection: five sixteenth-century panels that are on Germany's national heritage list. Executed by the Renaissance artist Bernhard Strigel, court painter to the Emperor Maximilian, they depict scenes from the life of the Virgin. The panels were originally commissioned for the monastery at Salem, and they have now been reunited in the Badisches Landesmuseums with the altarpiece of which they formed a part.

The sale was announced to the press at the beginning of July and soon attracted enthusiastic worldwide coverage. Shortly afterwards, Sotheby's experts finished cat-aloguing the estimated 7,000 lots, encompassing nearly 25,000 objects; it had taken six months. The catalogue was produced in boxed sets of seven volumes, full of historical information and illustrated with over three thousand colour photographs. It also included evocative sepia prints found in attics and cellars. These were taken in the 1890s and show many of the main rooms in the family's estates at the height of their grandeur.

Bidding on the first day of the auction established a pattern for the next fourteen days of the sale, as most estimates were doubled and trebled. Items that achieved particularly high prices included a silver-gilt table clock and tankard, made in 1697 by the Viennese sculptor Ignaz Elhafen, that was probably presented by the Holy Roman Emperor Maximilian to his military ally the Margrave Ludwig Wilhelm.

On the second day a record for eighteenth-century porcelain was set by a group of ninety 'Venetian Carnival' figures from the Ludwigsburg factory; then a new record for Meissen porcelain was achieved on day three by a 1740 'Insect' tea service, made for the Margravine Caroline Luise. By the end of the first week, the original estimate for the auction of DM36 million had been exceeded.

The total figure, DM77,586,739, set a new record for a sale held on a private estate, and in the end, over seventy percent of the collection remained in Germany. Prince Bernhard and his family were 'absolutely delighted with the outstanding result of this sale and overwhelmed by the amount of interest that it has generated throughout the world'.

Not only was the auction a success in terms of the prices achieved and the number of objects that were returned to their historic venues, but it gave the Margrave and his advisors the opportunity to review the substantial remainder of the Grand Ducal Collections. In November 1995 – just a year after Sotheby's were first brought in to discuss the sale – a Sotheby's team was advising on the integration and display of the many works of art that were retained from Neues Schloss and will continue to enhance the family's collections for generations to come.

LASTING IMPRESSIONS
NOTES ON A COLOURFUL CAREER

Michel Strauss

BY THE END OF THE nineteenth century the Impressionists were selling their work to collectors on both sides of the Atlantic and establishing an active and fascinating market in contemporary art. Superb collections have since been formed around the world. It is not difficult to account for the huge popularity of Impressionist paintings: the subjects – contemporary landscapes, portraits and still lifes – are reflections of the everyday, without religious, allegorical or mythological associations. Colourful and easy to appreciate, Impressionist paintings have been readily accessible through public museums and exhibitions for many years. Today, fine Impressionist paintings are still available although privately owned great works become rarer as more enter public collections. Regular international sales in Europe and America continue to excite the interest of collectors, dealers and museums in ever widening circles.

Worldwide economic and political changes have all had an impact on the art market in general, but the demand for Impressionist works in particular has remained strong and continues to grow. Whereas Paris and New York had been the major markets for Impressionist auctions in the 1920s, 30s and 40s, Sotheby's broke the mould in 1958 when we obtained for sale the Jakob Goldschmidt collection of seven masterpieces by Manet, Renoir, van Gogh and Cézanne. This event, the first of three that were to influence significantly the development of the Impressionist art market, marked the beginning of a forty-year period of enormous change. Later, in 1980, the Henry Ford sale produced the first multi-million dollar prices for art; then, at the end of that decade, the

The 1958 Goldschmidt sale of Impressionist masterpieces marked the beginning of the highly publicized international art auction.

Japanese buying frenzy showed the profound effects of unbridled speculation on a market.

The Goldschmidt sale was the first important Impressionist auction held in London, and it achieved higher prices than had ever been seen before. Peter Wilson, then Chairman of Sotheby's, created a grand event through the use of clever public relations and worldwide media coverage. Of course, sales in Paris, New York and other places had been advertised before, but never on such an international scale. Indeed, aided by the free movement of money in and out of England, the Goldschmidt sale marked the emergence of Sotheby's in London as a new centre for the international Impressionist market, and set a precedent for art auctions in general.

Working for Sotheby's for the last thirty-five years, I have had the privilege of being involved with some of the great Impressionist collections, the personalities behind them and the many record-breaking sales themselves. During my first year as a cataloguer (1961–2), we were consigned the Somerset Maugham collection of Impressionist and Modern pictures. I was working at that time alongside Bruce Chatwin, who later became a highly esteemed writer. He had already been with Sotheby's for a year as a cataloguer in the department and initially there was some rivalry between us, but within a few months we were able to develop a very good working relationship. He was a fount of knowledge and had great curiosity for the works of art of many cultures. This and the opportunity to view so many different, exciting sales each week had a profound influence on me.

The Maugham sale was my first experience with a great collection, and there were many more to follow. The first collection I catalogued myself, in 1962, belonged to Sir Alexander Korda, the film director/producer. The highlight was undoubtably van Gogh's

Van Gogh's Jardin public à Arles *made $5,830,000 in the 1980 Henry Ford sale, the first auction in which prices surpassed $5 million. It had previously been sold in the Goldschmidt sale for £132,000.*

Renoir's La Promenade, *the highest selling work from the 1989 British Rail Pension Fund sale, was bought by the J. Paul Getty Museum for £10,340,000.*

OPPOSITE: *At the landmark Goldschmidt sale, Sotheby's chairman, Peter Wilson, takes bids for Cézanne's* Garçon aux gilet rouge, *which sold for £220,000, more than twice the previous record for a painting at auction.*

ravishing still life of blue gloves lying next to a basket of lemons, which he painted in Arles in 1888. A stunning juxtaposition of yellow, blue and green, this was the first picture I had catalogued that I really fell in love with. Fortunately, I have the ability to remember most of the pictures I have worked with over the years and when visiting a collector's house I often find myself saying, 'Oh, there's one of my children, I sold it in 1965,' or some such, remembering the details of its history. Certain pictures will stay in my mind forever.

In 1978, after the death of Robert von Hirsch, a famous collector in Basel and very old friend of Peter Wilson, Sotheby's was asked to auction his varied collections. Over the years, since 1968, I had prepared insurance valuations for him. At first, he thought I had over-valued some works and asked me to substantiate the values by auctioning a painting by Signac in our London sale. I had valued it for £25,000 and, to my relief, it sold for £35,000 and earned his trust in my estimates.

It was a great joy to be shown the many treasures around the house. Each room was devoted to a different area. The Impressionists were in the living room, twentieth-century works in the dining room, Renaissance paintings in the library, and there was the greatest collection of nineteenth- and twentieth-century drawings and watercolours imaginable in his study. His was probably the finest collection in quality and variety seen at auction since the 1920s. In Impressionism, the works on paper were probably the most exceptional, in particular the van Goghs and Cézannes, most of which sold for record prices.

Two years later, the auction of the Henry Ford Collection took place in New York. This was the next Impressionist auction, after the Goldschmidt sale, to change the focus of the market. It included ten major Impressionist paintings, and, for the first time, prices passed the $5-million mark. Van Gogh's *Jardin public à Arles* made $5,830,000, a breakthrough in the perceived value and importance of works of art. Although the Goldschmidt sale had been a great success, many collectors tended to sell their pictures on the private market, believing they could get a better price and avoid the uncertainty of an auction. The Ford sale showed that such pictures could fetch quite exceptional prices and that there were

numerous collectors and museums eager to compete in the saleroom. It also demonstrated that even in times of economic and political crisis, great pictures would fetch great prices.

For me personally, the next really exciting event was the British Rail Pension Fund sale. In 1974 the managers of the Pension Fund decided to invest a small part of their annual income in the art market, using Sotheby's as their principle advisors. I was the main consultant for Impressionist and Modern paintings. In every significant international sale for five years, I chose works that I thought were suitable and submitted them to a panel of Sotheby's experts who, after consideration, would pass them on to the British Rail committee. The committee then confidentially decided which paintings to bid on. The Fund had chosen a good time to enter the market, as prices in the mid- to late 1970s were at quite reasonable levels.

In the late 1980s the Pension Fund decided to start selling groups from their collections. They thus consigned twenty-five Impressionist paintings for sale in the spring of 1989. These were works that I had chosen personally, so the group had the feel of a private collection. The timing was excellent; it was at the height of a tremendous boom in prices, fuelled largely by a thirst for Impressionist pictures by Japanese speculators. This influenced the overall market, and, although no Japanese bought in this sale, European and American collectors bid very strongly. Some of the paintings fetched twenty or thirty times their purchase price from only ten or fifteen years before. The Pension Fund had spent £3.5 million buying the paintings and their sale realized £35 million. The highlights were an early Renoir, *La Promenade,* bought by the Getty Museum for £10,340,000; a superb van Gogh drawing of cottages which made £2,310,000 and one of Cézanne's greatest still life watercolours, which realized £2,530,000. These last two had been in the Robert von Hirsch sale eleven years earlier, fetching £225,000 and £330,000 respectively.

So the market has indeed remained strong over the past thirty years in spite of a number of crises; however, the taste and demand for Impressionist paintings has shifted. For example, in the 1960s the early works of the greatest artists were considered the most important

and desirable. Paintings from the 1860s and 70s were bought by museums, collectors and dealers, who were quite dismissive about later paintings, such as Monet's waterlillies, Degas' dancers and bathers of the 1890s and the overblown pink and orange nudes painted by Renoir in the last fifteen years of his life. This trend began to change in the 1980s. Museums and scholars began to look at the later periods in a different way, organizing such exhibitions as *Monet in the 90s* and *Cézanne: The Late Work,* which were both huge successes in the 1980s, and continuing with *Degas: Beyond Impressionism,* being shown in London and Chicago this year.

There is not an inexhaustible supply of fine pictures and rarity adds to their value. In the Impressionist and Modern market there is little scope for discovery of unknown works. Durand Ruel, that prince of dealers who acted for most of the Impressionists, photographed all pictures that passed through his Paris gallery from the 1870s onwards. Many artists continued this practice on their own behalf and thus very good photographic records exist. Any discoveries would be of minor works, or perhaps pictures that had been given by artists to friends, or works on paper that were not photographed.

This is not to say that we do not rediscover works that have been lost to view for a very long time. One of the best recent examples is Monet's painting of poplar trees, *Peupliers au bord de l'Epte,* part of a series that he painted in 1891. Bought by a Swiss collector in the 1920s it only came to light seventy-five years later when the owner's family decided to sell it. It had been in an exhibition in Switzerland in 1952 but since then had disappeared from view. Though it was estimated at £2-3 million, it sold in London in June 1994 for £4,480,000, a price comparable to those achieved by similar Monets at the height of the 1980s' boom, which demonstrates that collectors will pay a significant premium for a work that is totally fresh on the market.

Impressionist paintings have generally been bought by European and American collectors and latterly by the Japanese who, since the 1980s, have had an enormous influence on the market. Between 1988 and 1990 prices of some Impressionist paintings were almost doubling every year. By 1990, works by many artists, especially those most admired by the Japanese – Monet, Renoir, Gauguin, van Gogh, Picasso, Matisse – were fetching prices that went beyond reason. But at the end of 1990 the bubble burst. Tax and fraud investigations caused the Japanese collectors to lose heart. Prices fell for two to three years and reached a low point in 1992. In 1993 the Impressionist and Modern market started to recover and top quality works began to make significant prices again. Now in 1996 we are beginning to see the return of a few Japanese collectors. Pictures of the finest quality are often reaching the old levels due to increasing rarity. Cézanne's *Nature morte: les grosses pommes,* which sold for $28,600,000 in May 1993, and Picasso's *Angel Fernandez de Soto,* which realized $29,152,500 in May 1995, are evidence of this.

The huge rise in the value of Impressionist paintings since World War II has obviously had a major impact on the international art market as a whole. It is a reflection of how highly art is valued and of the vast fortunes that have been made in the postwar period. Whereas in the early decades of this century people on relatively modest salaries could buy a work by contemporary artists such as Picasso, Klee or Kandinsky, today's equivalent works are, relative to salary, far more expensive, especially for younger collectors. The great industrialists of the recent past – Samuel Courtauld, Paul Mellon, Norton Simon, Peter Ludwig – created wonderful collections that have been passed on for posterity, and as works change hands at auction new collections will be formed.

However, the whole philosophy of collecting is complex and people collect for different reasons. In 1963, for example, I was involved in the sale of property belonging to an extraordinary Scottish collector, William T. Cargill. He was a lone bachelor living in a baronial house outside Glasgow, and when he died his executors discovered that all of his pictures remained unpacked, in their original crates, some stored underneath his bed. Although very eccentric, he had bought wonderful works with great discrimination. For him the pleasure was in having them, not in showing them. That attitude may seem strange, but I know other collectors who have bought important paintings over the years and keep them stored in warehouses or bank vaults, visiting them only on rare occasions. It is their secret passion and, for them, owning the works is what gives them satisfaction.

The Impressionist and Modern art market is healthy today. There is much interest both from collectors who have been buying for the past twenty years and from those who are new to the market. As our June 1996 sale in London proved, the Impressionist market is still a vital and stimulating area, and with pictures of the best quality, the excitement of the saleroom and high prices will always ensue.

There are few undiscovered great Impressionist works. Monet's painting of poplar trees on the Epte caused a stir in the art world when it reappeared on the market after 75 years.

Opposite: *Sotheby's most recent sale of Impressionist paintings in London, June 1996, produced the highest total of any sale of Impressionist and Modern pictures in London since April 1990. Cézanne's* Grands arbres au jas de bouffan *(shown here) realized £5,171,500.*

STARS OF THE SEASONS
THE ALLURE OF FINE JEWELS

David Bennett

FOR TWENTY YEARS, working at Sotheby's as an expert, jewellery has never ceased to fascinate and enthral me. Few objects are as personal or as individual as a jewel: turn over an early Victorian brooch and one will often find, engraved indistinctly on the back, a name and a date surrounding a small lock of hair belonging to the beloved. For a second, it is as if a curtain is drawn back slightly, and we glimpse the intimate, sentimental world of our ancestors, as clear as the crystal chandeliers, as exotic as the rich dark silk of a dress.

Sometimes a more recent past is recreated. It is December 1986 and my colleagues and I are sitting in the vault of the Banque de France in Paris. The first of the astonishing jewels the Duchess of Windsor had placed there before her death is passed to me from the imposing red leather jewel box bearing her monogram. I spend several minutes studying the superb workmanship and design, the fine quality of the stones until, turning it over to examine the back, I am a little shocked to find, written in facsimile of the Duke's hand, the poignant, unexpected phrase: 'We are ours now' and the date 1936. Many other pieces bearing different inscriptions follow, building up an intimate picture of their relationship, each event in their lives together marked by the gift of a jewel. This biographical aspect of the Duchess of Windsor's collection made the preparation of the catalogue such an immense pleasure, and contributed so much to the outstanding success of the sale – still unsurpassed today in the field of jewellery.

Sometimes one is fortunate enough to have the intimate nature of a jewel related at first hand. I am reminded of a very elegant London drawing room not far from the Brompton Oratory. It is late summer. Beside me on the chintz sofa a still resplendent, but rather tired and unwell, Ava Gardner is explaining how she

bought the emerald ring I am holding, set with a stone of the richest, purest green. This was the first of several meetings that spread into the autumn, and as each jewel was shown to me some other aspect of her colourful life would be recalled to her and revealed to me. It was a great privilege for me, and so deep a sadness that she did not live long enough to see the enormous success of the sale.

Some collections tell of a family tradition and history. In the case of the outstanding princely jewels of Thurn und Taxis, which we had the great good fortune to auction in 1992, the narrative illustrated in the pieces spanned several centuries. Not for a very long time had such a rich and varied collection of antique jewels been offered at auction. The pieces ranged from spectacular eighteenth-century bejewelled badges of the Order of the Golden Fleece, to the wedding tiara of Empress Eugénie made by Lemonnier in 1853 with pearls and diamonds from the State Treasury of France. This splendid jewel was purchased

Van Cleef & Arpels emerald-and-diamond cluster ring from the Ava Gardner collection, which sold for £209,000 in 1990.

Opposite: *The pearl-and-diamond tiara made by Gabriel Lemonnier in 1853 for the Empress Eugénie sold for SF935,000 in the 1992 sale of the Thurn und Taxis Collection in Geneva.*

Cecil Beaton's photograph of the Duchess of Windsor wearing a Cartier ruby-and-diamond bangle and her emerald-and-diamond engagement ring, which were included in the sale of her jewels held by Sotheby's, Geneva, in 1987.

The sapphire-and-diamond bracelet by Van Cleef & Arpels, inscribed 'For our contract 18-v-37' and given to Wallis Simpson by the Duke of Windsor two weeks before their marriage.

by the Louvre and many other pieces from the collection are now in German museums.

Of course, gemstones themselves hold their own romance and unique beauty; at their finest they exhibit a perfection unmatched in the natural world and evoke a primeval awe in us all. Over the years I have been lucky to have handled some of the greatest stones in the world and I am reminded of the belief in India that simply to touch a fine gemstone brings good fortune, so highly are they regarded.

Each for me has its own character and personality, and each is firmly fixed in my memory: the extraordinary emerald given by Queen Elizabeth I to the owner's ancestor in recognition for bringing back the first turkeys from the New World; the magnificent treasures of Nawabs and Maharajahs, redolent with Indian mystery; the fabled pearls of Barbara Hutton that were once fed to a goose to improve their lustre; the Rockefeller sapphire, the blue of an evening sky and of such unmatched purity it produced gasps of awe in seasoned gem dealers; a Burmese ruby that seemed to burn with an interior fire as if still hot from the inner reaches of the earth; the exquisite tiny blue diamond I discovered in a tobacco tin mixed in with worthless gaudy pastes, for which the owner had been offered £10 – its sale enabled him to purchase the retirement home of which he and his wife had dreamed.

In the last six years I have had the honour to sell the three most valuable stones ever to appear at auction. All three were diamonds over one hundred carats in weight (about the size of a small hen's egg), of the finest colour and purity, and each, serially, established a new world record price for a precious stone. The most recent, sold in Geneva in May 1995, was a superb pear-shaped stone of serene beauty, purchased by Sheikh Ahmed Fitaihi for the astonishing sum of $16.5 million after an unforgettable saleroom battle. The stone had never been worn and, indeed, had only recently been cut. Immediately after the sale Sheikh Fitaihi announced that he had named the stone 'Star of the Season' and as such it now enters the list of the great diamonds of the world alongside the Jonker and the Koh-i-Noor.

The staggering sums paid for these diamonds would have been unimaginable twenty years ago. Indeed, it is only in the last ten years that hitherto unknown large diamonds (over fifty carats) have begun to appear at auction. Cutters began to realize the advantage of exposing these extremely rare treasures to an international audience through the extensive Sotheby's network of clients and offices, which spans all the world's major economic centres. The growing strength and importance of buyers from the Middle East, particularly Saudi Arabia, following the oil crisis of the early 1970s, injected welcome new life into the precious stone market as, at the same time, America and Europe slipped gently into recession. More recently, Southeast Asia, especially Hong Kong, Singapore and Indonesia, is proving to be an important source of new collectors.

In jewellery the last twenty years have seen the emergence of a great interest in past designs. By the late 1970s, the art deco style, and jewellery of the 1920s and 1930s in general, was firmly established as a collectors' field with special interest paid to the splendid creations of the great French jewel houses such as Cartier, Van Cleef & Arpels, Boucheron, Mauboussin and Lacloche, and other jewellers with identifiable styles and designs who signed their work. In the 1980s, postwar jewellery was revived, and more recently, in line with dress fashions, so are the hippie-influenced creations of the early 1970s – which is exactly where I started all those years ago.

Opposite: (enlarged) The pear-shaped 'Star of the Season' diamond, weighing over 100 carats, was bought by Sheikh Ahmed Fitaihi for $16.5 million in 1995, the world-record price for a precious stone at auction.

SOTHEBY'S
at Auction

THE FINE ARTS

Old Master Paintings

Jacob van Ruisdael
**River Scene with a Waterfall
and a Large House**
Signed
Oil on canvas, 68.6 x 53.3cm (27 x 21in)
New York, $772,500 (£502,125) 11.1.96

It has been suggested that this work dates
from the early 1670s, after Ruisdael had
begun to combine powerful and significant
forms in both the near and middle distance.
The motif of moving water and waterfalls
derives ultimately from the painter Allart
van Everdingen. Ruisdael adopted the motif
as well as the format of the vertical canvas in
the early 1660s and continued to experiment
with it throughout the 1670s.

Valentin de Boulogne
The Crowning with Thorns
Oil on canvas
1.46 x 1.73m (4ft 9½ x 3ft 6¼in)
New York, $882,500 (£573,625) 11.1.96

Painted in Rome and showing the influence
of Caravaggio, this is among Valentin's
earliest known works. The subject of *The
Crowning with Thorns* was particularly popular with artists in Rome during the first half
of the 17th century, and Valentin executed
four different versions. It is the claustropho-
bic, confrontational violence of the painting
that engages the viewer. Valentin depicts the
sadistic crowning without pathos or melancholy, heightening the emotional impact
by means of the compressed composition
and the stark contrast of dark and light.

Francisco de Zurbarán
Christ with a Donor, 1640
Signed and dated
Oil on Canvas
2.46m x 1.67m (8ft x 5ft 5¾in)
Madrid, Pts 79,975,000 (£416,536; $629,724)
23.IV.96

This intense work was executed during
Zurbarán's most mature period and power-
fully reveals the sculptural quality of his style.
The modelling of the donor is highly
accentuated, and the white silhouette of
Christ is dramatically profiled against a dark
background, illuminated by a contrasting
shaft of light. The simple composition and
colours add to the profoundly contemplative
nature of the painting. Zurbarán remained
faithful throughout his life to the principles
of this solemn monumentality often under-
lined by an axis of violent light.

Francisco José Goya y Lucientes
The Death of a Picador, 1793
Oil on tinplate, 43 x 31.9cm (17 x 12½in)
London, £2,586,500 ($4,034,940) 3.VII.96
*From the Collection formed by the British
Rail Pension fund*

This small picture was painted when Goya
was recuperating from a serious illness
and marks a transition from the pleasant,
light-hearted subjects that had made him
so successful at court to a preoccupation
with a bleaker, darker world. It is one of a
series of 12, six of which depict bullfights.
Goya was an aficionado of the sport,
conveying in these works the excitement
of the crowd, an admiration for the skill
of the toreador, and above all, a profound
respect for the noble courage of the bull.

Frans Snyders
A Vendor of Fruits and Vegetables, 1627
Signed and dated '*Snÿders fecit, 1627*'
Oil on canvas, 1.65 x 2.42m (5ft 5¼ x 7ft 11¼in)
New York, $1,542,500 (£1,002,625) 11.1.96

Snyders was the doyen of Flemish still-life and animal painters.
Often sought out by his colleagues to execute elements of their
works, he collaborated with many artists, including van Dyck and
Rubens. Rubens' influence is apparent here, in the spirited design,
fluid touch and brilliant colour, as well as in the sheer audacity
of scale. Characteristically, the subject is abundance – the over-
whelming fecundity of nature – and the attendant potential for
prodigality. In this sense, it can be read as a *Vanitas*.

Pierre-Joseph Redouté
**An Elaborate Still Life of Flowers in a Glass Vase Resting on
an Alabaster Pedestal, with a Bird Nest and a Melon Below, 1796**
Signed and dated '*P. J. Redouté pinxit an 4*'
Oil on canvas, 99.1 x 80cm (39 x 31½in)
New York, $1,487,500 (£981,740) 16.v.96

This is a rare example of a work in oil by Redouté, who is best known
for his exquisite watercolours and engravings of plants and flowers.
He worked with the botanist Charles Louis L'Héritier de Brutelle
on a study of rare plants at Kew Gardens, was official painter for the
Musée National d'Histoire Naturelle, and was draughtsman to Marie
Antoinette. He also enjoyed the patronage of the Empress Josephine,
who employed him to make drawings of plants in the garden of
Malmaison.

Rembrandt Harmensz. van Rijn
Cupid Blowing a Soap Bubble, 1634
Signed and dated. Oil on canvas, 75 x 92.6cm (29½ x 36½in)
London, £3,851,500 ($5,892,795) 6.XII.95
From the Bentinck-Thyssen Collection

When Rembrandt painted this contemplative yet dynamic work,
he was living in Amsterdam and enjoying great success. Though the
figure is reclining, tension is created through dramatic light effects
and startling colour. The blowing of bubbles was a conventional
Vanitas emblem in Dutch 17th-century painting. By linking this
theme with Cupid, the artist symbolizes the transience of love.
The subject, unusual for Rembrandt, probably reflects the taste
of an unknown patron, but it is perhaps no coincidence that in the
same year, he married Saskia Uylenburgh.

Pieter de Hooch
A Maid with a Broom and a Pail in a Sunlit Courtyard, *c.* 1658–60
Signed with initials
Oil on canvas, 48.2 x 42.9cm (19 x 16¾in)
London, £2,201,500 ($3,434,340) 3.VII.96
From the Fattorini Collection

The pictures that de Hooch painted in his last years in Delft, and in
particular his courtyard scenes, have long been considered his finest
works. This one is typical of that group, brightly lit by summer
sunshine and composed so that the outside world is only admitted
through an open gate. Uniquely, however, the gate in this painting
reveals a farm landscape, and in the distance the twin towers of
a city that appears to be Delft, a poignant reference perhaps, to the
place he was shortly to leave.

Joos de Momper
Landscape with Harvesters *c.* **1625–30**
Oil on oak panel, 82 x 144cm (32¼ x 56in)
London, £793,500 ($1,214,055) 6.XII.95

One of the most successful and prolific landscape artists of his
generation in Antwerp, de Momper collaborated with many of
the outstanding figure painters of his day, including Teniers and
Brueghel. The large proportion of harvest scenes in his oeuvre
attests to the popularity they evidently enjoyed among his patrons.
This was one of de Momper's last pictures on the subject and
is more atmospheric than his earlier works, the fluid brushwork
conveying the misty haze of a hot summer's day.

Willem van de Velde the Younger
**A Calm, with a Dutch Smalschip Alongside a Kaag
at Anchor in the Foreground and an English Man O' War
at Anchor Beyond**
Signed '*W. V. V.*'
Oil on oak panel, 50.8 x 45.5cm (20 x 18in)
London, £1,376,500 ($2,147,340) 3.VII.96
From the Fattorini Collection

Although he painted calms sporadically throughout his career, van
de Velde specialized in this genre during the 1650s and early 1660s,
refining his technique throughout those years. Most of these pictures
are on a small scale, with carefully ordered compositions. The
absence of wind to disturb the sails or the surface of the water allows
the objects and their reflections to be painted in very sharp focus.
The only ripples are created by a school of dolphins just breaking
the surface.

Old Master Drawings

Albrecht Dürer
**The Holy Family Beneath a Tree,
a Castle in the Distance**
Inscribed with a fake monogram
Pen and brown ink, 22.8 x 14.6cm (9 x 5¾in)
New York, $244,500 (£156,480) 9.I.96

Comparable in technique and characteriza-
tion to a similarly early study of the Holy
Family in the British Museum, dated *circa*
1491, this drawing highlights Dürer's deep
admiration for Schongauer (*circa* 1450–91).
It has been extensively published over the last
90 years and the attribution to Dürer has, in
the past, been controversial, however recent
scholarship has confirmed the link with the
youthful studies that presage the engraving
of the *Virgin with Dragonfly,* dated *circa* 1495.

Jean Baptiste Oudry
**An Album of One Hundred and Thirty-
Nine Drawings for the Montenault Edition
of the *Fables of La Fontaine***
All but four signed and dated in pen
and black ink '*1729*', '*1730*' *or* '*1731*',
the frontispiece dated '*1752*'.
Each page *c.*30.8 x 25.5cm (12⅛ x 10in)
London, £551,500 ($860,340) 3.VII.96

The 139 drawings in this spectacular album
are among Oudry's greatest achievements,
bringing to life with immense wit and
charm the *Fables of La Fontaine*. In 1751
the artist sold the drawings to Monsieur de
Montenault, who used them as the basis for
the engravings illustrating his lavish edition
of the *Fables*. Kept in an album since the
mid-18th century, the drawings retain their
original freshness and the dazzling blue of
the paper itself.

British Pictures 1500 — 1850

Alexander Cozens
Coastal Landscape with Shipping at a Port
Oil on canvas, unlined, 64.5 x 89cm (25½ x 35in)
London, £162,100 ($256,118) 8.XI.95

Traditionally attributed to Richard Wilson, this painting has only
recently emerged as an early and rare oil by Cozens. It perhaps
dates from the 1750s or 1760s, after the artist's journey to Italy
in 1746. Cozens was one of the first British landscape painters
to make the pilgrimage to Rome to absorb the grand style of the
Old Masters and study classical antiquity. As in many of his works,
the sky is not painted naturalistically but to a 'system' simulating
hidden evening sunlight.

Attributed to Steven van der Meulen
Portrait of Queen Elizabeth I, *c.* 1567
Oil on panel, in a fine carved wood frame, 51.5 x 42cm (20¼ x 16½in)
London, £128,000 ($194,560) 3.IV.96

This portrait is one of the earliest sophisticated images of Elizabeth I.
When she succeeded her sister Mary in 1558, the court painter was
Hans Eworth. However, probably due to his religious affiliations,
Elizabeth appears to have avoided using his services. Early pictures
of the Queen were unflattering, mechanical workshop productions.
A proclamation was drafted to counter these debased images in 1563.
Circa 1567 Elizabeth sat for a new official pattern, of which this is one
of the finest examples.

John Frederick Herring, Snr
The Start of the Epsom Derby, 1835
Signed and dated
Oil on canvas, 110.5 x 157.5cm (43½ x 62in)
New York, $2,250,000 (£1,485,000) 12.IV.96
Property from the Succession of Blanche Sternberger Benjamin

Herring annually painted the Derby winners for his great series
of pictures. On this occasion he was requested by the distinguished
racehorse breeder John Bowes to paint a highly ambitious work
recording the start of the race. Herring was not only a brilliant
painter of horses, but also a shrewd businessman, and this painting
led to a series of important commissions from Bowes. The striking
composition shows the artist's ability to portray both the thorough-
breds and their jockeys in a range of positions and movements.

James Seymour
Sterlin, a Grey Racehorse Held by a Groom, 1738
Signed *'J Seymour Fecit 1738'* and inscribed
'Sterlin, a plate horse, which belongs to James Bisshopp, Esq'
Oil on canvas, 98 x 123cm (38½ x 48½in)
London, £419,500 ($637,640) 3.iv.96

This painting of the racehorse Sterlin forms part of the famous group
of pictures by Seymour commissioned by Sir William Jolliffe. Jolliffe
was Director of the Bank of England for many years and collected
an important group of sporting pictures that hung originally at
Epsom House. Plate horses were so named because they were
considered good enough to run the Royal Plates put up annually
by every sovereign from Queen Anne to Queen Victoria.

British Watercolours

George Housman Thomas
**The Coronation of the King and Queen
of Prussia on 18th October 1961 – A Set
of Four Watercolours, 1862**
Two signed, one: '*George Housman Thomas*',
the other: '*George H. Thomas 1862*'
Pen and brown ink and watercolour over
pencil heightened with bodycolour and gum
arabic. One, 34.5 x 50cm (13½ x 19¾in);
another, 34 x 53.5cm (13½ x 21 in); another,
33.5 x 47.5cm (13 x 18¾in); the other,
48 x 33.5cm (19 x 13¼in)
London, £89,500 ($138,725) 11.VII.96

Thomas was commissioned by Queen
Victoria to go to Königsberg to record the
coronation of King William I and Queen
Augusta of Prussia. Her daughter, married
to the Crown Prince of Prussia, wrote to
Victoria: 'Mr Thomas has made some
charming sketches…' This is the most
spectacular of the four, giving a panoramic
view of the courtyard while the King
acknowledges the cheering crowd. The
others show soldiers in the parade ground;
the King proceeding down the walkway after
the ceremony, and the Coronation banquet.

Joseph Mallord William Turner, RA
Nineveh, Moussul on the Tigris, *c.* **1833–35**
Watercolour heightened with bodycolour,
gum arabic and scratching out
12.5 x 20.5cm (5 x 8in)
London, £63,100 ($99,698) 9.XI.95

This is one of 26 drawings commissioned
from Turner by the engravers Edward
and William Finden between 1833 and 1836.
John Ruskin, who 'discovered' Turner
and championed his work, described these
as 'quite unrivalled examples of his richest
executive powers on a small scale'. Turner
produced his watercolours of the Holy Land
from the sketches of travellers. This example
shows the modern town of Moussoul and
the two mounds on either side of the Tigris
said to contain the ruins of Ancient Nineveh,
the capital of Assyria.

Victorian Pictures

James Jacques Joseph Tissot
Preparing for the Gala
Signed
Oil on canvas, 86.4 x 41.9cm (34 x 16½in)
New York, $1,817,500 (£1,199,550) 23.v.96

This is amongst Tissot's most beautiful and
inventive English pictures. Set in his garden
in St John's Wood, the work may well have
been painted to mark the completion of
the handsome new pool and colonnade that
became a favourite setting for his domestic
works. But it is the flags that give the composition its heraldic brilliance and Japanese
flavour. Uncharacteristically for Tissot, the
painting exists in two quite different versions;
the other, now called *Still on Top*, is in the
City Art Gallery in Auckland, New Zealand.

Ford Madox Brown
The Last of England, 1852–5
Oil on panel, oval, 19.5 x 17.5cm (7¾ x 6¾in)
London, £155,500 ($247,245) 6.XI.95

Completed in 1855, *The Last of England* is one
of the best known images in Victorian art.
It deals with emigration, a subject that had
personal significance for Brown. Describing
himself as 'intensely miserable very hard up
& a little mad' at this time, he had considered
moving to India. The successful sale of the
picture for which this is the coloured sketch
meant that he could stay. Thoroughly documented in Brown's diary, this study appears
to have existed unrecognized since 1868.

Modern British Paintings

Laurence Stephen Lowry, RA
A Cricket Match, 1938
Signed and dated
Oil on canvas, 45.5 x 61cm (18 x 24in)
London, £282,000 ($437,100) 19.VI.96

Lowry's love of sport, particularly football and cricket, is reflected in a small number of pictures of professional and domestic sporting events. Alick Leggart, Treasurer of Lancashire County Cricket Club, remained a good friend of the artist for many years. Here, he locates the game in the backstreets of 1930s Manchester, the setting for his most famous works. The resulting picture is a typically sensitive piece of social observation, tenderly celebrating community life.

Frank Bramley, ARA
Delicious Solitude, 1909
Signed and dated
Oil on canvas, 121.9 x 91.4cm (48 x 36in)
New York, $613,000 (£404,580) 23.V.96

A genre and portrait painter, Bramley was a leading member of the Newlyn School, Cornwall. He was also a founder of the New English Art Club, formed in 1886 and patterned after the French *Salon des Refusés*. Other founding members included George Clausen and James McNeill Whistler. After 1897 Bramley increasingly turned to portraiture. In 1909 this work was exhibited at the Royal Academy, where it was warmly received by critics and public alike.

William Scott, RA
Colander, Beans and Eggs, 1948
Signed
Oil on canvas, 66 x 81.5cm (26 x 32in)
London, £89,500 ($138,725) 19.VI.96

Scott said of his work in the latter half of the 1940s, 'I picked up from the
tradition of painting in France that I felt most kinship with – the still life
tradition of Chardin and Braque, leading to a certain kind of abstraction
which comes directly from that tradition'. This work reflects that kinship
whilst retaining Scott's highly individual style, combining the sensual use
of colour and paint with a stark simplicity of composition that anticipates
the later abstract works.

19th-Century European Paintings

Ignacio Zuloaga y Zabaleta
Corrida de Toros en Eibar, 1899
Signed
Oil on canvas, 2 x 1.49m (6ft 6¾in x 4ft 11in)
New York, $1,075,000 (£677,250) 1.XI.95

This painting of Zuloaga's birthplace is the only documented Basque townscape by the artist. It has been suggested that it was made during his extended wedding trip when he and his bride, Valentine Dethomas, visited Eibar in the province of Vizcaya. The work depicts a place of great symbolic value for Zuloaga and reflects his love of bullfighting. He once entered the bullring but gave up the sport after being severely gored.

Giuseppe de Nittis
La promenade à Hyde Park, 1876
Signed and dated
Oil on canvas
43.2 x 33cm (17 x 13in)
New York, $552,500 (£364,650) 23.v.96

In 1867, following the advice of his teacher
Jean-Léon Gérôme at the Ecole des Beaux-
Arts in Paris, de Nittis began to concentrate
his attention on the human figure. A decade
later he visited London and painted city
landmarks such as Westminster Bridge,
Trafalgar Square, Buckingham Palace and
several views of fashionably dressed figures
riding horses and strolling through Hyde
Park. Along with his works showing Parisian
street scenes, these paintings established de
Nittis as a fundamental chronicler of *belle
époque* society.

Emile Claus
La faneuse, 1896
Signed and dated
Oil on canvas, 130.2 x 97.5cm (51¼ x 38⅜in)
New York, $321,500 (£212,190) 23.v.96

From 1883, Claus worked at Astene, near
Deinze on the banks of the Lys, in an old
hunting pavilion that he later turned into
his home, *Zonneschijn*. It was here that he
turned to *plein-air* painting and his work
started to show the influence of the
Impressionists. Later, *Zonneschijn* became
the centre for Flemish luminism. *La faneuse*
is an excellent example of the balance Claus
achieved between naturalism, the graceful use
of colour and the effects of light and shadow.

Jean-Léon Gérôme
The Accepted Prayer, *c.* **1890–95**
Signed
Oil on canvas, 76.8 x 100.3cm (30¼ x 39½in)
New York, $1,075,000 (£709,500) 23.v.96

Gérôme often made trips to Cairo during his youth. He is first recorded as having visited the Mosque of Quait Bey, the highly praised Cairene monument depicted here, in 1868. In this work he combines his admiration for the Muslims' piety and for their ordered, geometrical architecture. Throughout all of his Orientalist subjects there is a great respect for the straightforward spontaneity of Muslim prayer. Strongly anti-clerical, Gérôme no doubt admired the independence of the worshippers.

Angelo Morbelli
An Elegant Lady on Lake Maggiore, 1915
Signed and dated
Oil on canvas, 58 x 103cm (23 x 40½in)
London, £441,500 ($679,910) 12.VI.96

In this work, Morbelli synthesized the Divisionists' views on colour. Using photographs to capture the effect of light, Morbelli aimed to adhere as much as possible to reality without distracting from the subjective qualities of the painting. Through the photographic nature of the composition and its analytical objectivity Morbelli achieves this realism. But the contemplative female figure and the acute contrast of light and shade also convey a wealth of emotion oscillating between subtle melancholy and languid abandon.

Jean-François Millet
L'été, les glaneuses, 1853
Signed
Oil on canvas, 38.1 x 29.2cm (15 x 11½in)
New York, $3,412,500 (£2,149,875) 1.XI.95

This is one of a set of paintings depicting
the four seasons and celebrating the tenuous
balance between labour and reward in the
precarious cycle of country life. The series
was commissioned by the Parisian architect
Alfred Feydeau and consolidated the creation
of Millet's mature Realist style. Concentrating
his understanding of rural life, his skill
as a draughtsman and command of colour
nuance, Millet created an image that has
come to symbolize the idea of work in the
Western imagination.

Ferdinand Hodler
The Woodcutter, 1910
Signed and dated
Oil on canvas, 128 x 105cm (50½ x 41⅓in)
Zürich, SF1,357,400 (£696,102; $1,078,958)
5.VI.96

In April 1908 the Swiss National Bank,
founded the year before, commissioned
Hodler to create designs for the 50- and
100-franc notes on the theme of 'Work in
Switzerland'. Hodler was at the height of
his career, having recently completed the
great mural for the new University of Jena.
For the 50-franc note he conceived this image
of a woodcutter which is amongst the most
fascinating representations of workers in
European painting.

Russian Art

The Protection of the Mother of God (Pokrov), 16th century
Perhaps Rostov or Vologda
107 x 83cm (42⅛ x 32¾in)
London, £78,500 ($120,105) 14.XII.95

Representations of two events, both celebrated on 1 October, are integrated in this composition. In the first, Saint Andrew the Fool (bottom right) points upwards to the apparition of the Virgin. She weeps and spreads her veil over the congregation of the Church of the Blachernae, Constantinople, to symbolize her protection of the city. Beneath her, in the second scene, Roman the Melodist, a hymnographer for the Church of the Divine Wisdom in Constantinople, holds a scroll inscribed with the Christmas Kondakion, which he is about to chant.

Art in Israel

Edouard Moyse
The Covenant of Abraham *c.* 1860
Signed and indistinctly dated
Oil on canvas, 58 x 86cm (22¾ x 33¾in)
Tel Aviv, $91,600 (£57,708) 12.x.95

This monumental composition is one of the most important paintings by a 19th-century Jewish artist of a Jewish subject to appear at auction in recent years. Moyse, born in Nancy in 1827, distinguished himself by applying his technical virtuosity to Jewish religious themes that had not been explored previously in art. This circumcision scene seeks to capture the timeless nature of the covenant of Abraham.

Impressionist & Modern Art

Claude Monet
Les Meules, Giverny, Effet du Matin, 1889
Signed and dated
Oil on canvas, 65.1 x 92.1cm (25⅝ x 36¼in)
New York, $7,152,500 (£4,720,650) 1.v.96

Monet's series paintings are not only masterpieces
of Impressionism but also significant precursors
of crucial developments in 20th-century art.
He embarked on the grainstacks, a group of thirty
paintings executed between 1889 and 1891, at a time
when Impressionism was going through a period
of transition. By doing so he revitalized the movement
whilst celebrating the timeless grandeur of the French
countryside. For the first time in his career, Monet
was established in the public eye as one of the great
contemporary painters.

Paul Gauguin
Femmes au Bord de la Rivière, 1892
Signed and dated
Oil on canvas
32 x 40cm (12½ x 15¾in)
London, £3,191,500 ($4,978,740) 27.XI.95

This work dates from Gauguin's first visit to Tahiti. He arrived in the idyllic province of Mataieia in 1891 in search of 'ecstasy, calm and art' and remained there for two years. His delight with the simple lifestyle, the beautiful natives and the sensual, tropical colours is palpable. Containing elements that recur in many subsequent paintings, this composition can be seen as a blueprint for Gauguin's Tahitian works. Warm orange-red tones and vibrant brushwork express the intensity of Gauguin's idealization of Tahiti and its 'noble savages'.

Paul Cézanne
Grands Arbres au Jas de Bouffan *c.* 1890
Oil on canvas, 73 x 59cm (28¾ x 23¼in)
London, £5,171,500 ($7,964,110) 24.VI.96

The Jas de Bouffan was an estate near Aix-en-Provence owned by Cézanne's father. It was here that the artist painted some of his greatest landscapes. Its tall, powerful trees lit by strong Mediterranean sunlight inspired in Cézanne a more ruthless investigation into the mechanics of composition than any yet undertaken by his contemporaries. In works such as this, in which Cézanne developed his idea that nature should be interpreted, not slavishly reproduced, he established a new, profoundly influential visual language.

Vincent van Gogh
Sous-Bois, 1890
Oil on canvas, 73.3 x 92.1cm (28⅞ x 36¼in)
New York, $26,952,500 (£16,980,075) 8.XI.95
From the Collection of Joseph H. Hazen

Unique among his late works, this painting conveys van Gogh's
delight in the cool interior of a grove of trees, a subject that had
always attracted him. It was painted in the artists' colony of Auvers,
whose surrounding countryside van Gogh found 'profoundly
beautiful'. In the 70 days spent at Auvers before his death, he produced as many canvases. Showing no trace of the troubled state of
mind that led to his suicide, this work is characterized by its lyricism
and rhythmic brushwork.

Georges Seurat
Le Chenal de Gravelines; Petit Port Philippe, 1890
Oil on panel, 15.9 x 25.1cm (6¼ x 9⅞in)
New York, $2,752,500 (£1,816,650) 1.v.96

This work was painted by Seurat in Gravelines, a seaport near the
French-Belgian border, whose obscurity apparently appealed to
the increasingly reclusive artist. It is a study for the third in a series
of paintings of Gravelines and offers many clues relating to the
evolution of the finished picture. The balance between the artist's
evident delight in the sunlit scene before his eyes, and the rigour
of his method gives this sketch in oils its particular charm.

Edouard Vuillard
Le Square Berlioz (La Place Vintimille), 1915 (reworked, 1923)
Signed
Distemper on canvas, 1.62 x 2.28m (5ft 4 x 7ft 6in)
New York, $3,082,500 (£2,034,450) 1.v.96
Property from the Estate of Lita A. Hazen

This panoramic view of Le Square Berlioz is one of Vuillard's most
comprehensive treatments of a favourite theme – the daily activities
in the small square outside his apartment on rue de Calais, Paris.
He lived there for 18 years, above the square that was known as the
Place Berlioz, after the statue of the composer, before its name was
changed to Vintimille, after the town of Ventimiglia on the Franco-
Italian border. A serene meditation, the work is painted with
imposing, formal design.

Pierre Bonnard
Interieur Avec des Fleurs, 1919
Signed
Oil on canvas, 116.2 x 89.2cm (45¾ x 35⅛in)
New York, $3,302,500 (£2,179,650) 1.v.96

Interieur Avec des Fleurs is characteristic of Bonnard's decorative,
intimate interiors dealing with memory and nostalgia. He creates
a careful balance between the spare geometric forms and predo-
minantly black and white colour scheme of the foreground, and the
exuberant, organic patterns and bright palette of the background.
By placing the flowers of the still life against the floral-patterned
wallpaper, Bonnard juxtaposes nature and art. Further dialogues and
contrasts are created between complementary and adjoining hues.

Pablo Picasso
Ma Jolie: Guitare, Bouteille de Bass,
Grappe de Raisin et Verre, 1914
Signed
Oil and sand, sawdust and coloured beads on board
51.4 x 67.5cm, (20¼ x 26½in)
New York, $6,162,500 (£3,882,375) 8.xi.95

The addition of sawdust, sand and glass beads to the surface of this wonderfully rich composition creates a sculptural presence. The year 1914 was an *annus mirabilis* for Picasso, both in terms of his personal life and the fertility of his art. His willingness to experiment with three-dimensional forms and a more colourful palette reflects his *joie de vivre*. Picasso dedicated this work to his lover Eva Gouel, the '*jolie*' of the title, and its exuberantly decorative, festive nature has been playfully described as 'amorous Cubism'.

Fernand Léger
La Pipe, 1918
Signed and dated
Oil on canvas, 90.2 x 71.1cm (35½ x 28in)
New York, $6,602,500 (£4,159,575) 8.xi.95
From the Collection of Joseph H. Hazen

La Pipe was painted during one of the most prolific and creative periods of Léger's career. Billowing clouds of smoke, contrasted with architectural surfaces, appeared frequently in his work of this time, as did the motif of the pipe. Invested with a deeply personal resonance for Léger, the pipe provided respite from the horrors of war. This painting marks a distinct shift in his work away from the imagery of the trenches, towards the aesthetic of the machine and the pristine postwar metropolis.

Marc Chagall
Les Amoureux, 1916
Signed, dated '916' and dedicated in Cyrillic,
'*for my wife*'
Oil on board, 70.7 x 50cm (27⅞ x 19⅛in)
London, £2,751,500 ($4,237,310) 24.vi.96

Painted during a blissful period in Chagall's
life, this work is a self-portrait of the artist
with his beloved wife, Bella, and is considered to be amongst his masterpieces.
One of four paintings of lovers made in 1916,
it is the only work in the group showing the
couple face to face. Utilizing a radical Cubist
fragmentation, Chagall paradoxically achieves
an unparalleled harmony and sense of elated
calm. His exploration of the colour blue,
which symbolized the spiritual for Chagall,
is exceptionally skilful.

Joan Miró
Trois Femmes, 1935
Signed, titled and dated '18.2.35'
Oil and sand on board, 106 x 75cm
(41¾ x 29½in)
London, £2,421,500 ($3,729,110) 24.vi.96

Painted the year before the outbreak of the
Spanish Civil War, this is one of Miró's most
striking works of 1935. The hard surface of
the masonite board is ideally suited to the
brilliant pigments and black enamel paint,
heightening the impact of the imagery.
Despite the large scale, the artist has painted
with the discipline of a miniaturist, his
precision contrasting sharply with the wild,
biomorphic forms. *Trois Femmes* was formerly in the collection of Alexander Calder,
Miró's lifelong friend and collaborator.

Carl Hofer
Festlicher Tag *c.* **1922**
Signed and titled
Oil on canvas, 130 x 104cm (51¼ x 41in)
London, £551,500 ($849,310) 24.VI.96

In the early 1920s Hofer began to develop
a unique, classic-romantic style that was to
set him apart from his fellow Expressionists,
such as Kirchner, Schmidt-Rottluff and
Kokoschka. There are few existing works
dating from 1921–22 and this is a powerful
and rare example of his early monumental
figure paintings. The composition, in which
the bodies of three women intertwine to
create a central, pyramidal form, is one of
Hofer's favourite groupings.

Paul Klee
Geschwister
Signed, titled and dated '*1930 e. 8*'
Oil on canvas, 70.7 x 45.2cm (27¾ x 17¾in)
London, £2,861,500 ($4,406,710) 24.VI.96

In the summer of 1929, Klee commenced
a group of works whose compositions were
based on superimposed or interlocking
planes. Whilst many of these are abstract,
others, like this one, introduce a charming
and witty human element suggested by a
few simple signs. Two pin-thin pairs of legs
create the impression of figures walking
harmoniously together. The dots and lines
for eyes and nose are simple but expressive.
The small red heart, doubling as a mouth,
is a symbol of sibling love.

Contemporary Art

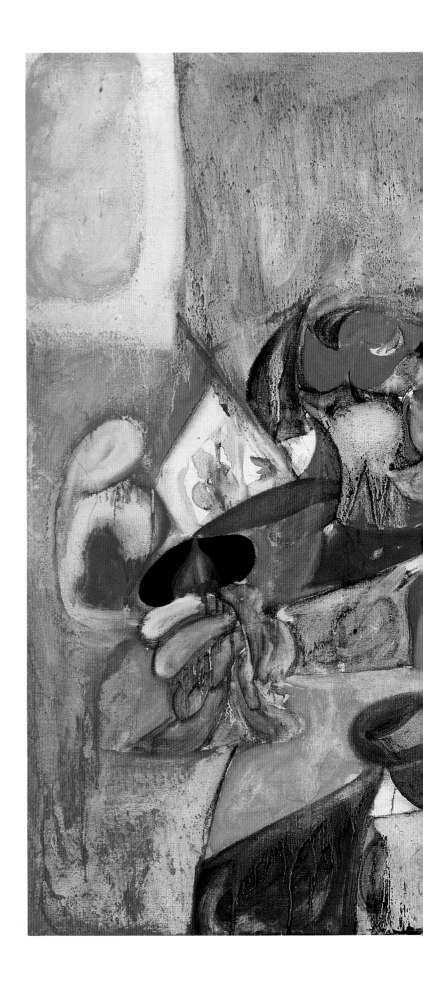

Arshile Gorky
Scent of Apricots on the Fields, 1944
Signed and dated
Oil on canvas, 78.7 x 111.8cm (31 x 44in)
New York, $3,962,500 (£2,536,000) 15.XI.95

This work, which represented a breakthrough
in Gorky's career, was sold in November 1995
for the highest price ever achieved by one of
his paintings. The style demonstrates his major
contribution to 20th-century art: he created
a bridge between the dreamlike landscapes
of Surrealism and the painterliness of the
Abstract Expressionists, whom he greatly
influenced. Based on the exiled artist's
memories of his Armenian homeland,
organic, erotic forms combine with veils of
rich colour in a composition pulsating with
nostalgia and sensuality.

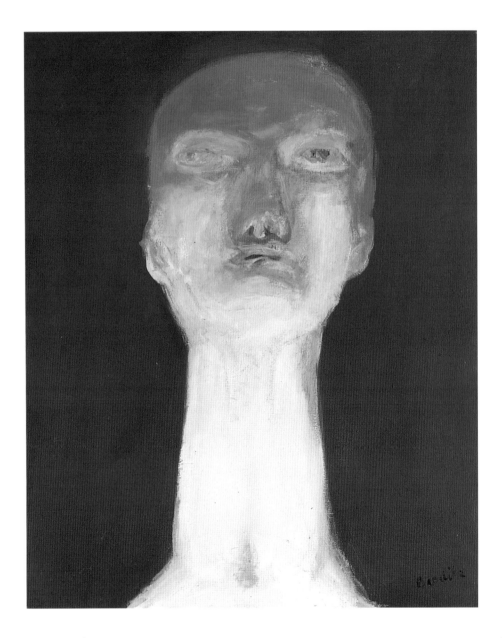

Georg Baselitz
E. N. Idol, 1964
Signed and titled
Oil on canvas, 100 x 81cm (39¼ x 31⅞in)
London, £232,500 ($358,050) 26.VI.96

This is a crucial work in the development
of Baselitz' mature style, painted in a year
of immense creative energy for the artist.
At the time, Baselitz was fighting an obscenity
charge in the Berlin courts for creating paintings that deliberately contradicted the values
of bourgeois Germany. This portrait calls
upon such diverse resources as Mannerist
painting, the drawings of the insane and
powerful sexual imagery to create a hallucina-
tory image of great force and presence.

Jean Dubuffet
Ils Tiennent Conseil, 1947
Oil on canvas, 145 x 112cm (57 x 44½ in)
London, £1,123,500 ($1,730,190) 29.XI.95

This is one of six paintings made by Dubuffet
on his return from El Goléa, an oasis in
the Algerian desert. It combines his familiar
'naive' style with a palpable awe for the mysticism of the Bedouin. Dubuffet's emphasis
on the terrain represents a significant
departure from his other desert paintings
in which vast skies predominate, and
presages his later geological pictures of the
earth. Using subdued colours, broken only
by the scorching yellow sun, he evokes the
dusty heat and mystery of the desert.

Emilio Vedova
Presenza, 1959
Signed, titled and dated
Oil on canvas, 120 x 120cm (47¼ x 47¼in)
Milan, ʟ170,800,000 (£73,662; $112,073)
28.v.96

Vedova was a founder member of the *Fronte Nuovo delle Arti* in 1946, and one of the 'Eight Italians' grouped together in the 1952 Venice Biennale. His painting is preoccupied with claustrophobia, and many of his works, both figurative and abstract, suggest a feeling of oppression and the effort to break loose from a world grown too small for his vision.

Gerhard Richter
Scheune (Barn), 1984
Signed, dated and numbered '550-1'
Oil on canvas, 95 x 100cm (37½ x 39½in)
New York, $965,000 (£617,600) 15.XI.95

Sold for a price that broke the artist's record, *Scheune* is based on photographs taken by Richter in the Bavarian Forest. In transferring the image onto canvas the artist aims to retain some of the qualities of photography, including any technical impurities. But this is not a literal exercise in verisimilitude.

The brushwork is evident in the feathery treatment of the vegetation, and the luminous quality of the daylight is more akin to the artificial beauty of 19th-century landscape painting than to documentary realism.

Eva Hesse
Sans II, 1968
Fibreglass and polyester resin
one of five units
96.5 x 218.4 x 15.6cm (38 x 86 x 6⅛in)
New York, $662,500 (£437,250) 8.v.96

Sans II, a major statement of Post-Minimalist art, was sold for a
record figure in May 1996. It was part of a series made for Hesse's
first one-woman show, *Chain Polymers*. The linked, repeated modules
reflect the chain-like, molecular structure of the industrial polymers
she employed as media – latex, fibreglass and polyester resin.
True to her characteristic harmonization of opposites, the surface
both refracts and absorbs the light, and the sculpture combines hard,
impersonal materials with the soft translucence of a honeycomb.

Jasper Johns
Winter, 1986
Signed and dated
Encaustic on canvas, 190.5 x 127cm (75 x 50in)
New York, $3,082,500 (£1,972,800) 15.XI.95
From the Collection of Mr and Mrs Asher B. Edleman

Winter is the final piece of the *Seasons*, Johns' seminal quartet
of autobiographical paintings dealing with the theme of the Stages
of Man. The life-size silhouette is traced from a template of the
artist's own shadow. Representing the later stages of life, the work
is full of references to Johns' past oeuvre, including a fragment
of stripes from one of his signature flag paintings and the black,
white and grey palette prominent in his compositions of the
1950s and 60s.

Andy Warhol
Mao, 1972
Signed
Acrylic and synthetic polymer silkscreened
on canvas, 208 x 142cm (82 x 56in)
London, £672,500 ($1,035,650) 26.vi.96

Mao is a classic emblem of Pop Art, conveying the iconic monumentality and painterly
inventiveness of Warhol at the height of his
celebrity. Inspired by Richard Nixon's historic
trip to China, the artist turned to the icon of
proletarian culture, Chairman Mao Tse-tung.
At the time, Warhol was enjoying the full-
scale benefits of Western 'decadence'. Such
irony is typical of Warhol's social commentary and attitude to fame, which is also
evident in his depictions of Marilyn Monroe,
Elvis Presley and Jacqueline Kennedy.

Lucio Fontana
Concetto Spaziale 'Jazz', 1956
Signed and dated
Oil, mixed media and glitter on canvas,
69 x 55cm (27¼ x 21⅝in)
London, £188,500 ($290,290) 26.vi.96

Exuberantly conveying the mood of jazz,
this spectacular early work contrasts colours
and shimmering silver glitter to create an
exhilarating and rhythmical image of musical
energy. For Fontana the circular form represented a pivotal energy source, and here, the
spinning, spherical element is reminiscent of
a fiery planet, while the swirling trails, traced
in the glitter of the yellow background, recall
a meteorite disappearing into the atmosphere.

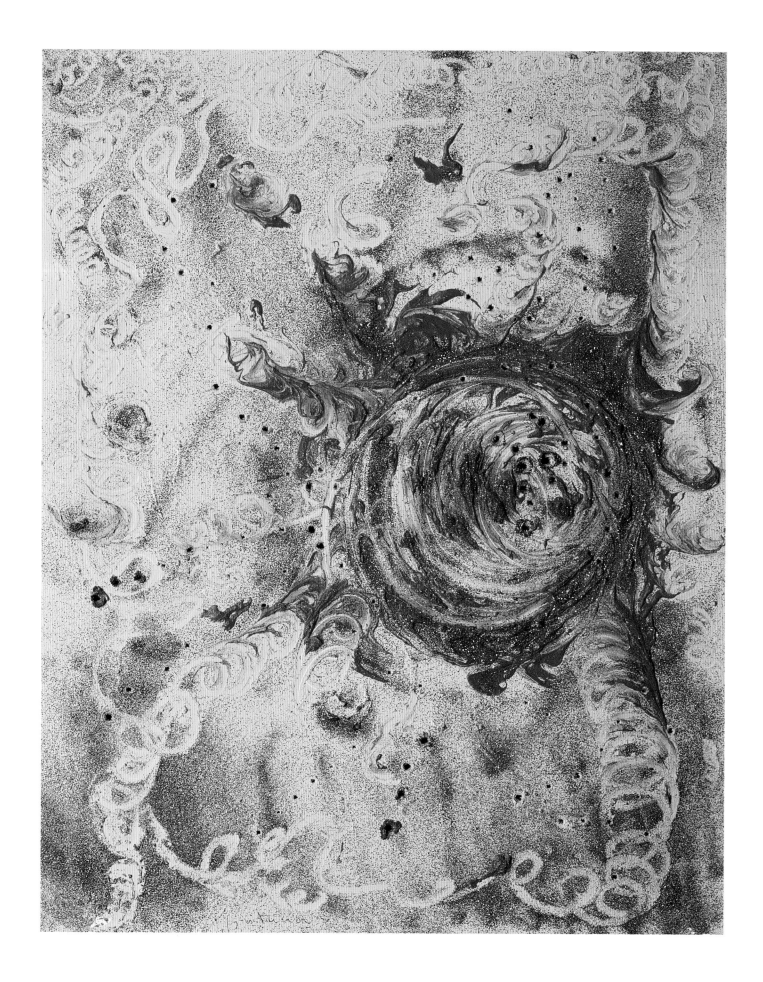

Irish Art

Jack Butler Yeats, RHA
A Farewell To Mayo, 1929
Signed
Oil on canvas, 61 x 91.5cm (24 x 36in)
London, £804,500 ($1,214,795) 16.v.96

This painting was a gift to Vivien Leigh from her husband, Laurence Olivier. One of the earliest major works executed in Yeats' distinctive late Expressionist style, it is a study of emigration and loss. A lone traveller and his silent driver head for Galway or Sligo to board the ship for America. Behind them, lit by the yellows and crimsons of the setting sun, lies the emigrant's last glimpse of Mayo, which is among the poorest and the most beautiful counties of Ireland.

Scottish Pictures

William McTaggart, RSA, RSW
A Highland Burn, 1877
Indistinctly signed and dated
Oil on canvas, 81 x 90cm (32 x 43in)
Gleneagles, £58,700 ($90,985) 29.VIII.95

McTaggart's work was of seminal importance in the development of Scottish art. He specialized in figure paintings, landscapes and seascapes. The way in which these children playing in a brook merge with their surroundings reflects McTaggart's familiar theme of man's unity with nature. The artist started work on this painting during a visit to Whitehouse in 1874. It was much admired by Sir James Guthrie, PRSA, who encouraged the *Scottish Arts Review* to illustrate it as a full-page plate in 1888.

American Paintings

Maxfield Parrish
Daybreak, 1922
Signed and dated
Oil on panel, 67.3 x 115.6cm (26½ x 45½in)
New York, $4,292,500 (£2,833,050) 22.v.96

Before Parrish had even begun this extraordinary painting, he called it his 'Magnum Opus'. It became the most successful work of his career. Commissioned for reproduction as a print, it was offered to the public in 1923. The response was unprecedented – it was purchased by an estimated one in four households in America. Enchanting Arcadian subject matter, breathtaking scenery and meticulous attention to detail account for its popularity. The remarkable luminosity and purity of colour, achieved through the layering of transparent glazes, became the hallmark of Parrish's style.

John Singer Sargent
Capri Girl (Dans les Oliviers, à Capri) 1878
Signed and inscribed
'*To my friend Mrs Sorchan*'
Oil on canvas, 77.5 x 63.5cm (30½ x 25in)
New York, $4,842,500 (£3,196,050) 22.v.96

This work was painted on the island of Capri, off the coast of Italy. At the age of 22, Sargent was already on the brink of a successful career. The girl is Rosina Ferrara, who became Sargent's favourite model during his stay. Self-assured and sensual beyond her 17 years, she epitomized the exoticism and freedom that Sargent celebrated in his early Mediterranean genre pictures. At one with nature, she leans against the gnarled trunk of a tree. The loose brushwork and warm, golden hues capture the soft glow of sunlight illuminating the olive grove.

Norman Rockwell
The Watchmaker, 1948
Signed
Oil on canvas, 66 x 66cm (26 x 26in)
New York, $937,500 (£618,750) 22.v.96

Though Rockwell established his reputation as an illustrator with covers for the *Saturday Evening Post*, he also produced advertisements for more than 150 companies during his career. This commission for The Swiss Federation of Watchmakers was considered by Rockwell to be one of his best. The detail of the cluttered shop, combined with an idealized view of childhood in small-town America, is typical of his work. *The Watchmaker* was sold for the highest price ever achieved for one of his paintings.

Frederick C. Frieseke
In the Garden, Giverny, *c.* 1910–12
Signed
Oil on canvas, 81.3 x 81.3cm (32 x 32in)
New York, $1,020,000 (£663,000) 29.XI.95

This picture of the artist's wife is one of a number of vibrant summer paintings in which Frieseke experimented with pattern, colour and design through the depiction of the natural world. The extraordinary sense of sunlight is achieved in a number of ways.

In full bloom, the garden is depicted as a two-dimensional, decorative plane, as if flattened out by the glare of the sun. The luminous tone of the lilies and their shadows, cast onto the translucent parasol and hat brim, enhance this effect.

Martin Johnson Heade
Seascape: Sunrise, 1860
Signed and dated
Oil on canvas, 71.1 x 127cm (28 x 50in)
New York, $910,000 (£600,600) 22.v.96

This painting is a major recent discovery from Heade's
early period. One of his first, pure, large-scale seascapes,
it constituted an important development of his basic theme
– the large, curling wave. The rough surf, breaking against
the rocks, contrasts with a calm sky, tinged with the pink
and lavender hues of dawn. Heade's exploration of light
and his depiction of atmospheric effects at different times
of the day later earned him a reputation as one of the most
original painters working in the luminist vein.

Maurice Prendergast
**Rainy Day, Siena (Campo Vittorio
Emanuele, Siena)** *c.* **1898–9**
Signed
Watercolour on paper, 47.6 x 33cm (18¾ x 13in)
New York, $937,500 (£618,750) 22.v.96

The spectacular light and picturesque buildings of Italy
captivated Prendergast during a pivotal trip in 1898–9.
The result was a series of dazzling watercolours depicting
religious processions, secular parades and crowds of locals
and tourists against the background of scenic architecture.
This work captures the decorative effect of rain on the
crowded, earth-coloured streets of Siena – a subject
ideally suited to the translucent medium of watercolour.
An excellent example of Prendergast's best period, it
beautifully demonstrates his approach to elevating the
ordinary occurrences of daily life.

Latin American Paintings

Frida Kahlo
Los cuatro habitantes de México, 1937
Signed and dated
Oil on masonite, 31.4 x 47.9cm (12⅜ x 18⅞in)
New York, $882,500 (£582,450) 14.v.96

Like many of Kahlo's works, this is a powerful exploration
of self identity. The child-like Frida is surrounded by three
folk-art icons and a Nayarit Pre-Columbian statue, representations of real objects owned by her husband, Diego
Rivera, and symbols of their Mexican heritage. Apart from
these figures, the austere town square is abandoned, said
Kahlo, 'because too much revolution has left Mexico
empty'. In 1938, the artist gave the painting to her friend
Ella Wolfe, in whose collection it remained until it was
sold in May 1996.

Diego Rivera
En el viñedo, 1920
Signed and dated '20'; also signed and dated on the reverse
Oil on canvas, 67.3 x 48.9cm (26½ x 19¼in)
New York, $827,500 (£529,600) 21.xi.95

Sensual oranges and russets evoke the ripe fecundity of
autumn. These colours and the style of the painting recall
the work of Renoir, to whom Rivera was perhaps paying
homage. He came into contact with the French master,
along with other eminent avant-garde artists, when in 1907
he travelled to Europe from Mexico. The work he produced
during the fourteen years he was there reflects these
influences. Later he rediscovered his native traditions,
particularly the art of the Mayas and the Aztecs, and
liberated himself from European influences.

Leonora Carrington
**Les distractions de Dagobert
(Pleasures, Etc.), 1945**
Signed and dated '*1945 September*'
Egg tempera on masonite, 74.9 x 86.7cm
(29½ x 34⅛in)
New York, $475,000 (£304,000) 21.XI.95

This is one of the most significant works by British-born artist Leonora Carrington to have come to light in recent times. An imposing picture utilizing complex layerings of space and multiple perspectives, it serves as an archetypal statement of Carrington's key psychological and visual concerns. Numerous figures, some human, some animal, others weird and wonderful hybrids, are participants in a dream-like fantasy of the pleasures of the flesh. Highly imaginative, sexually-charged and enigmatic, this is a masterpiece of Surrealism.

Claudio Bravo
Fantasma de un supermercado, 1969
Signed and dated *'MCMLXIX'*
Oil on canvas, 111.4 x 140.3cm (43⅞ x 55¼in)
New York, $299,500 (£197,670) 14.v.96

This painting is one of a series depicting mundane objects, executed in the 1960s when the Chilean-born artist was living in Madrid. With his wrapped package and supermarket pictures, Bravo became an integral part of the 'New Realist' group that flourished in the Spanish capital at this time. Though he has approached his subject matter in a quasi-spiritual style, drawing on the tradition of the Spanish still life, these works also illustrate Bravo's unique appropriation of North American Pop Art.

Canadian Art

Cornelius David Krieghoff
A Winter Incident
Signed
Oil on canvas, 30.5 x 40.6cm (12 x 16in)
Toronto, CN$77,000 (£36,000; $57,000)
15.XI.95

This charming work was previously unrecorded, having been in a private family collection before it was brought to auction. Krieghoff was a German painter who lived in Canada from 1840–66, settling near Montreal in 1849. There, and in Quebec (1853–66), he painted the Indians, French Canadian life and the landscape in a dramatic, often anecdotal style. His pictures, which demonstrate an eye for detail and a taste for brilliant colours, were sought after by the English garrison at Quebec as souvenirs.

Australian Art

Sir George Russell Drysdale
West Wyalong, 1949
Signed
Oil on composition board, 80 x 110cm,
(31½in x 43⅓in)
Melbourne, AUS$855,000 (£401,850; $624,150)
21.VIII.95

West Wyalong has been described as 'one of the most melancholy but loveliest of all Drysdale's images of a country town'. Devoid of people, and illuminated by the setting sun, the street resembles an empty stage set. The light that shines from a single doorway reinforces the sense of loneliness and poignancy.

Influenced by the vogue for photographing Australian towns and cities, the painting was included in Drysdale's 1949 solo exhibition in Sydney, where it attracted wide critical acclaim.

Prints

Rembrandt Harmensz. van Rijn
Woman Bathing her Feet at a Brook, 1658
(enlarged)
Etching printed with plate tone on a cool-
toned Japan paper, 15.9 x 8cm (6¼ x 3⅛in)
New York, $112,500 (£75,375) 3.v.96

Truly early impressions of the etching *Woman
Bathing her Feet at a Brook*, such as this
superb example, are very rare. It is one
of a group of drawings and prints depicting
female nudes created by Rembrandt at the
end of his career. These late studies concentrate on the subtle play of light and shadow
over a monumental, almost classical, female
form. In this example, the colour of the paper
and the rich tone lend a mysterious quality
to the simple subject.

Albrecht Dürer
Melencolia I, 1514
Engraving. A very fine Meder IIA impression
24.2 x 19cm (9½ x 7½in)
London, £65,300 ($100,562) 25.vi.96

In Dürer's lifetime his fame was spread
abroad mainly through the wide circulation
of his engravings and woodcuts in which he
had made unprecedented technical advances.
Increasingly difficult to find in fine early
examples, *Melencolia* is a celebrated and mysterious allegory that associates a melancholic
disposition with the artist's vocation.

Mary Cassatt
The Letter, *c.* 1891
Signed in pencil and inscribed
'Imprimé par l'artiste et M Leroy, (25 épreuves), serie ? unique'
Drypoint, soft-ground and aquatint printed in colours, inked
à la poupée, a very fine fresh impression of the third state,
on J. Whatman paper with the watermark *'1861'*
34.6 x 22.8cm (13⅝ x 9in)
New York, $316,000 (£211,720) 4.v.96

This work is characteristic of Cassatt's highly individual use of
Japanese styles and subjects. Not only does she base the design and
composition on Japanese woodcuts, but she also draws on common
Asian themes. One of a series of ten works suggesting different times
of day – morning and bedtime rituals, afternoon socializing, evening
entertaining – it recalls many similar Japanese surveys of women's
daily lives. The emphasis on quotidian scenes and gestures also
underscores Cassatt's affinity with Impressionism.

Giorgio Morandi
Natura Morta con il Panneggio a Sinistra, 1927
Signed and dated in pencil, numbered *'37/40'*
Etching, second state of two, on wove paper
34.7 x 49.6cm (13⅝ x 19½in)
London, £52,100 ($79,713) 1.XII.95

The gentle humanity of Morandi's oeuvre owed much to his native
town of Bologna, whose quiet seclusion and long creative tradition
were major factors in his artistic development. Taking simple,
everyday objects, he invested them with a new metaphysical reality.
His lyrical, purely visual pictures, which consist almost entirely
of still lifes and landscapes, were the result of his engrossment in
objective and pictorial reality. This etching demonstrates his great
skill as a graphic artist.

Pablo Picasso
**Buste de Femme d'Après Cranach
le Jeune, 1958**
Linocut printed in colours, signed in blue
crayon, numbered '*15/50*', on sturdy Arches
paper, 64.5 x 53.4cm (25⅜ x 21in)
London £194,000 ($298,760) 26.VI.96

In 1958 Picasso moved from Paris to the
South of France. There, he no longer had
access to the print ateliers of the capital.
Frustrated by having to wait for proofs
from Paris, Picasso developed an alternative,
the linoleum cut, to create his coloured
images. The linoblock was soft and malleable,
allowing the cutting of fluid strokes, as well
as the possibility of printing layers of colour.
This virtuoso work was his first major
achievement in the medium.

Jasper Johns
Ale Cans, 1964
Lithograph printed in colours, signed
in pencil, dated and numbered '*15/31*',
on handmade Japan paper, with the blind-
stamp of the publisher, '*ULAE*'
36 x 28cm (14⅛ x 11in)
New York, $101,500 (£68,005) 5.V.96

Ale cans were amongst Johns' iconic subjects,
which also included lightbulbs, flags, targets,
numbers and flashlights. His treatment of
these common items confused their familiar
meanings and specific identities. His central
theme, through which he challenged accepted
associations and ways of seeing, was the
relationship between the object itself and his
rendering of it. This image of cans standing
on a plinth is not a representation of real
beer tins, but a portrait of one of his own
bronze sculptures.

Photographs

[Attributed to John Plumbe, Jr]
The United States Capitol, *c.* 1846
(enlarged)
Half-plate daguerreotype, in one half
of a leather case with hanging ring
New York, $189,500 (£119,385) 5.x.95

This superb image, one of only three known
daguerreotypes of the United States Capitol,
is believed to be by John Plumbe, Jr. It shows
the East front of the building as it appeared
circa 1846, with the White House in the distance at left. The earliest extant photograph
to include both buildings, it depicts the
Capitol as it was when the young Congress-
man Abraham Lincoln first arrived in
Washington. It achieved a world record
price for any 19th-century photograph sold
at auction.

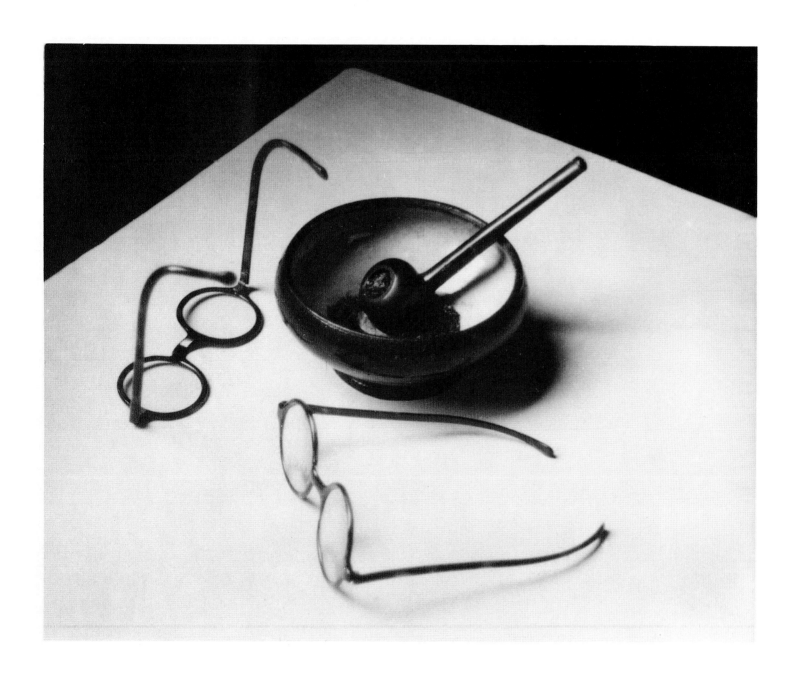

André Kertész
Mondrian's Glasses and Pipe, 1928
(enlarged)
Reverse annotated in pencil '*Chez Mondrian Paris 1928*', and in ink '*Foto: André Kertész*'
Silver print, 9.5 x 11.4cm (3¾ x 4½in)
London, £65,300 ($97,297) 2.v.96

André Kertész was an expatriate Hungarian living in Paris. He made this poignant work when he was invited by the editor Michel Seuphor to photograph Mondrian's studio and home. The arrangement of the artist's trademark pipe and glasses captures his spirit with great economy in an image that lies somewhere between a still life and a portrait. Two years earlier, Kertész had made *Chez Mondrian*, a simple, perfectly balanced photograph of the hallway in the painter's studio that became one of Kertész' most famous compositions.

LITERARY PROPERTY

Books and Autograph Manuscripts

il funt inimicū · fed aliuß quidā cucurrit volenß ipfū defedere
et armauit fe verfuß iimicoß illiuß Illi autē dixerūt Amice tibi
iuriā non facim9 · tolle qð tuū eft et vade qm de iimico noftro
vindictā qrim9 Qui nō acqefciß fermonib9 eoz ad bellū cōtra
eoß fe parauit Illi autē idignati cū iimico ipfū mutilauerunt

De elephāte q̄ genua nō flectit Dyalog9 octuagefim9non9

Elephaß vt bzito dicit dicit² ab elephio grece qð mōß
latine dicitur ppter magnitudinē cozpiß Hoc genuß
animātiß in rebuß bellīciß aptū eft In hijß animalib9
parfe et medi ligneiß turribuß collocatiß tāq̄ de muro iaculiß
dimicāt Intellectu et memozia nulla vigēt gregatim incedūt ·
motu quo valeant · murem fugiūt Biēnio poztāt fetuß nec
ampliuß q̄ femel gignūt nec plureß fed tātum vnū gignūt · vi-
uūt ad tricentoß anoß vt dicit pfi · ethp xiiij° · ¶ Narrat fcrip-
tura que cōtinet veterū hiftoziaß q̄ elephaß hōc modo capitur
Due puelle virgineß vberibuß et fupiozi pte cozpiß nudate p-
gunt vbi habitant elephanteß vna earū vznā altera gladium
feriß · quibuß alta voce cātātibuß audit elephaß accurrit ppe
Qui mox naturali inftinctu vgineß carniß inocenciā recognof
renß in eiß caftimoniam veneratur · lambenfq̄ earum pectuß
et vbera et delectatuß mirifice refoluitur in fopozem nec more puellaz puella cū gladio tenez pfodienß vitrem elephātiß
fanguinē ruetiß fundit Excipitq̄ in vzna puella altera fanguinē quo regaliß purpura tingitur Hic cum fit inter feraß

f z

Dialogus creaturarum moralisatus, 1480
(by Mayno de Mayneriis?)
Gouda, 3 June 1480
Gerard Leeu, first edition
New York, $525,000 (£330,750) 1.XI.95
From the Collection of Otto Schäfer

This book stands alongside the fables of
Aesop and Bidpai as one of the three great
illustrated fable-texts of the early years of
printing. Whereas the Aesop and Bidpai texts
were taken up by a wide variety of publishers,
the success of *Dialogus creaturaram* is very
closely focused on Gerard Leeu, and on
the anonymous artist who designed the
exceptionally fine and humorous outline
blocks. The publication was issued in
Gouda, Antwerp and Delft in Latin, Dutch
and French.

Giovanni Boccaccio
De casibus virorum illustrium
(French, tr Laurent de Premierfait)
De la ruine des nobles hommes et femmes
Bruges, 1476, Colard Mansion, first edition
New York, $690,000 (£434,700) 1.XI.95
From the Collection of Otto Schäfer

This luxury publication venture between
Colard Mansion and an unknown artist is
the first printed book to include engravings.
Only three remaining copies contain the
illustrations. The sole work printed by
Mansion that clearly precedes this text is
the *Jardin de dévotion*, whose colophon
states that it is '*Primum opus impressum
per Colardum mansion*'.

¶ Bocace commence ici son
tiers liure. dont le premier
chappitre est un petit prolo=
gue en admiration .

Consueuere longu
ac laboriosu iter,
etc. Ceulx qui
font long chemyn
et laborieux ont acoustume

non pas seulement arrester
aucunes fois, torchier leurs
sueurs, alegier les corps, pre
dre le vent soef et par bruuai
ges oster le soif: mais ilz ont
acoustume aussi puis qu'ilz ont
tourne le visatge derriere de
mesurer les espaces qu'ilz ont
passees recorder les chasteaux
et raconter les fleuues: Les

הָא לַחְמָא עַנְיָא רִי אֲ
אֲכָלוּ אַבְהָתָנָא בְּ
אַרְעָא דְמִצְרָיִם
כָּל דִכְפִין יֵיתֵי וְיֵכוֹל
כָּל דִצְרִיךְ יֵיתֵי וְ
וְיִפְסַח הָשַׁתָּא הָכָא
לְשָׁנָה הַבָּאָה בְאַרְעָ

Haggadah
Prague, 1526, Gershom Cohen
New York, $277,500 (£174,825) 1.XI.95
From the Collection of Otto Schäfer

A landmark in Hebrew books, this is the earliest illustrated *Haggadah* and a work of extreme rarity. In 1514, Gershom Cohen established Prague as the first city north of the Alps to have an important Hebrew press. His descendants continued in a printing dynasty that lasted for well over two centuries. The 1526 *Haggadah* was Gershom Cohen's masterpiece, beginning a tradition for illustrated *Haggadot* that continues unbroken to this day.

[Oeuvres]
Giovanni-Battista Piranesi and Francesco Piranesi
Paris, 1804–1807, 26 volumes in 25, uniformly bound
in red straight-grained half morocco gilt by Tessier
London, £133,500 ($204,255) 30.XI.95

Giovanni-Battista Piranesi (1720–78) trained as an architect but is perhaps better known for his etchings of Italian antiquities and ruins. In his controversial publication *Della magnificenza ed architettura de' Romani* (1761) he boldly asserted the superiority of Roman (Etruscan) architecture over Greek. This illustration depicts the Piazza Navona in Rome.

[Mary Annette Beauchamp Russell]
**The Complete Set of 16 Fine Ink and Watercolour Drawings
by Kate Greenaway for** *The April Baby's Book of Tunes*
London, £45,500 ($70,525) 21.XI.95

Apart from the illustrations to *The Queen of the Pirate Isle,* this is
the only complete set of drawings for a book by Kate Greenaway.
It was her last to be published, appearing in 1900 with the illustrations reproduced actual size. The pictures show three young girls
in six different situations and ten scenes from nursery rhymes
preceded by manuscript music. The illustration below depicts Curly
Locks washing dishes while her admirer offers a present through
the open window.

Pierre-Joseph Redouté
**Les Liliacées. 8 volumes, text by Augustin-Pyramus
de Candolle (Vols I–IV), François Delaroche (Vols V–VI)
and Alire Raffeneau-Delile (Vols VII–VIII)**
Paris, 1805–1816 [1802–1816]
Chez L'Auteur ... De L'Imprimerie de Didot Jeune
New York, $360,000 (£234,000) 5.VI.96

This rare issue of Redouté's masterpiece is one of four surviving
examples that include an extra suite of plates. The illustrations
were executed by means of stipple engraving, an ideal method for
rendering the subtle gradations of tone found in Redouté's watercolours. To achieve the best results, a number of black impressions
would be struck to take the edge off the plate before printing in
colours. These 'Special Issues' with the extra suite of black
impressions were apparently bound in a very small number.

François Marie Arouet de Voltaire
Zadig ou la destinée
Paris, 1893, Imprimé pour Les Amis des Livres
London, £23,000 ($35,650) 21.XI.95

This edition of *Zadig ou la destinée* contains
eight colour-printed etchings after J. Garnier,
F. Rops and A. Robaudi and is in an elaborate
Art Nouveau-style binding by Marius Michel.
The father-and-son firm of Marius Michel
initially worked in the historical styles that
were favoured in the 19th century. This
naturalistic floral design, composed of
coloured morocco onlays, is typical of their
later output and reflects much of the orna-
mental work at the turn of the century.

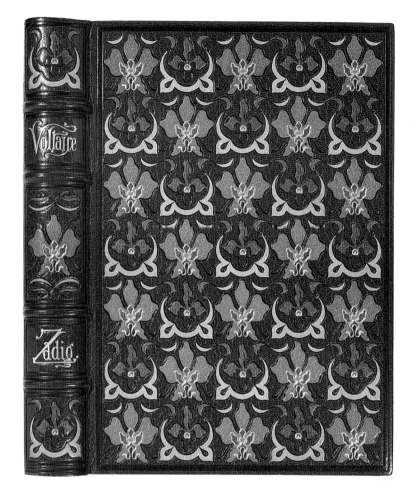

Charles Hersent
Optati Galli de cavendo schismate
[Paris], 1640
Bound with another work
London, £25,300 ($38,709) 8.XII.95
From the Collection of Otto Schäfer

This celebrated Parisian mosaic binding is
one of the finest and most elegant examples
of 18th-century inlaid work. It is unsigned
but classified among the '*premières reliures*'
of Antoine-Michel Padeloup le jeune. The
painted ovals appear to be a unique feature.
Hersent's text is of outstanding rarity, having
been deliberately destroyed on the orders of
Cardinal Richelieu.

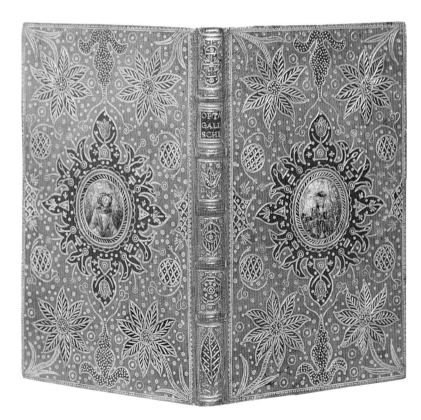

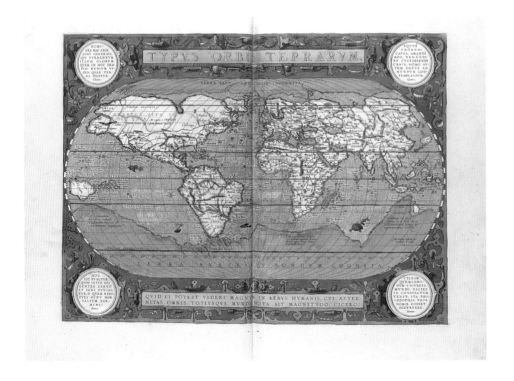

Abraham Ortelius
Theatrum orbis terrarum
3 parts in one volume, Latin text edition
London, £121,400 ($186,956) 27.VI.96

A record price was obtained for this edition
of the '*Theatrum*' with 146 map sheets in full
contemporary colour. The maps were bound
in elaborately tooled blue morocco by Roger
Bartlett, one of the outstanding binders of the
period. Leaving London after the Great Fire
of 1666, Bartlett set up a business in Oxford,
where he executed de luxe presentation
bindings for the university and colleges.
This atlas was last sold in June 1940 at
Sotheby's for £42.00.

Willem and Jan Blaeu
Le Grand Atlas, ou Cosmographie Blaviane
Amsterdam, 1667
Johannes Blaeu, second edition,
French text 12 volumes with woodcuts
New York, $255,500 (£166,075) 5.VI.96

A superb example, this famous atlas is
beautifully coloured in a contemporary
hand and contains 21 supplementary maps.
Conceived as a luxury product by the father
and son team of Willem and Jan Blaeu, it
came to represent the 'Golden Age' of Dutch
achievement and was presented to important
foreign dignitaries throughout Europe. Some
300 sets are believed to have been published
and form one of the greatest cartographic
publishing ventures of all time.

Vincent van Gogh
Autograph Letter to Albert Aurier
Signed in French, 2 pages
27 x 21cm (10⅝ x 8¼in)
New York, $107,000 (£69,550) 12.XII.95

In an article in the *Mercure de France* of
January 1890, the art critic Albert Aurier
published a lengthy and complimentary
commentary on van Gogh's work. Here,
the artist expresses his thanks and praise
of the critic's own writing, stating that
'I rediscover my canvases in your article'.
Letters by van Gogh are extremely rare
at auction, and this example is the most
significant written during his stay at the
asylum at Saint-Rémy-de-Provence from
July 1889 to mid-April 1890.

Erich Maria Remarque
**Autograph Manuscript of *Im Westen
Nichts Neues* (All Quiet on the Western
Front), in German**
c. 1927–28, *c.* 120 pages
London, £276,500 ($423,045) 1.XII.95

All Quiet on the Western Front is probably
the best known anti-war novel of the century.
It has enjoyed phenomenal success both
as a book and a film and has been translated
into some 45 languages, selling an estimated
50 million copies worldwide. This is the first
manuscript of a major 20th-century novel
to appear on the market since Kafka's
Der Prozess in 1988, and is the only known
complete text in the author's own hand.

Music Manuscripts

Giuseppe Verdi
Otello
Autograph sketch of Act IV Scene I
20 pages (one blank), oblong folio, with a
presentation inscription from Maria Carrara
Verdi to Giulio Gatti-Casazza, between
December 1884 and mid-September 1885
London, £188,500 ($288,405) 1.XII.95

This hitherto unknown and undocumented
autograph working manuscript for *Otello*
contains complete drafts of the original
versions of the *Willow Song* and *Ave Maria*.
These include substantial amounts of new
material which in many respects differ
from the known versions. It is the most
important Verdi item ever to have been
offered at auction.

Fryderyk Chopin
Nocturne
Autograph manuscript of the *Nocturne
in C minor, Op.48 No. 1* and the *Nocturne
in F sharp minor Op.48 No.2*
20 pages in all (14 with text and notation)
oblong folio, signed
London, £188,500 ($288,405) 1.XII.95

This manuscript is the only surviving
autograph of these two Nocturnes, which are
among Chopin's greatest and most celebrated
works. It appears to be the last remaining
manuscript of compositions in this genre
that will ever come on the market. The
deeply tragic, passionate and noble *C minor
Nocturne* is one of the composer's greatest
works. The autograph manuscript is as
dramatic and vivid as the music itself.

Johann Sebastian Bach
Autograph manuscript of the cantata
'Ach Gott vom Himmel sieh darein', BWV 2
Leipzig, June 1724
12 pages, folio, unbound
c. 35.5 x 21cm (14⅕ x 8⅖in)
London, £496,500 ($749,715) 15.v.96

This cantata dates from J. S. Bach's second
year as cantor for St Thomas's, Leipzig. The
text is based on Martin Luther's paraphrase
of Psalm 12. One of the last complete Bach
manuscripts remaining in private hands,
it is a rare document, as it contains sketches
by the composer in the margins, some of
them in organ tablature. Under great pressure
from his employers, Bach would produce
these works at the rate of about one a week.
Nevertheless, this detailed score, probably
a first draft and heavily revised in places,
provides a unique insight into his perfect-
ionist approach.

Eigitur cl
sime pater
xpm filuu
dim nrm
rganmsa
uti accepta

et benedicas hec ✠ dona. hec

hec sancta ✠ sacrificia illibata

mus que tibi offerim' p ecclia tu

Western Manuscripts

Missal, in Latin
Northeastern France (diocese of Soissons), *c.* 1250–75
Illuminated manuscript on vellum, 33.4 x 22cm (13⅛ x 8½in)
London, £364,500 ($554,040) 18.VI.96

Mass was celebrated daily in the Middle Ages but relatively few
manuscript missals have survived, and a complete, richly illuminated
Gothic missal of the 13th century is a great rarity. This large manuscript was made for a church in the diocese of Soissons and is
illustrated with 23 miniatures in colours and highly burnished gold.
It is from the castle library of Beloeil in Belgium and was sold by
order of His Highness the Prince de Ligne.

Book of Hours, in Latin
Rome, *c.* 1480–85
Illuminated manuscript on vellum
12.3 x 8cm (4⅞ x 3⅛in)
London, £31,050 ($47,196) 18.VI.96

This tiny *Book of Hours* was probably illuminated by a French artist
in Italy – its miniatures mingle French and Italian elements.
The artist is known as the Master of the della Rovere Missals because
of his work for Domenico della Rovere (d. 1501), archbishop of Turin.
It is likely that he was working in the papal court in Rome by the
late 1470s. His style shows the influence of Jean Fouquet, and there
is circumstantial evidence for identifying him with the painter
Jacques Ravaud.

Book of Hours, in Latin
Bourges, *c.* 1500
Illuminated manuscript on vellum
17.7 x 11cm (7 x 4⅓in)
London, £33,350 ($51,026) 5.XII.95

This *Book of Hours* was illuminated in Bourges by the artist known
as the Master of the Lallemant Boethius, and includes 13 large
miniatures with wonderful borders, often containing naturalistic
flowers. Several of the miniatures, such as the one shown here,
include tiny blue shields inscribed '*M.D.*' These may be the painter's
initials, or more probably, the date 1500, in Roman numerals.

Historia Calamitatum and **The Love Letters**
of Abelard and Heloise, in Latin
France, first half of 14th century
15.2 x 9.5cm (6 x 3¾in)
London, £34,500 ($52,785) 5.XII.95

The love story of the philosopher Peter Abelard (1079–1142) and
Heloise (*c.* 1100–1164), is probably the greatest of the Middle Ages.
The two met while Abelard was teaching at Notre-Dame in Paris.
When Heloise became pregnant, a scandal ensued. Abelard was
captured and castrated and Heloise was sent to a nunnery. Abelard
wrote a heart-rending account of his life, the *Historia Calamitatum*,
which inspired the infinitely tragic letters that passed between the
lovers over many years. This is one of only twelve known copies of
the texts.

Oriental Manuscripts and Miniatures

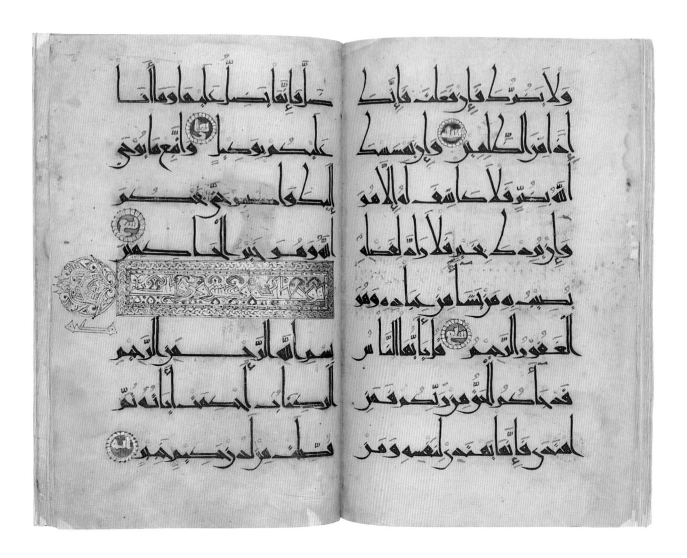

An Important Eleventh Century Qur'an Section
Illuminated Arabic manuscript in *'Eastern Kufic'*
script on thick paper
Fatimid, North Africa, probably Cairo or Qairawan
52 leaves, 8 lines to a page
35.9 x 23.4cm (14⅛ x 9¼in)
London, £73,000 ($114,610) 18.x.95

The large size of this Qur'an allows for elaborate illumination
throughout the manuscript, including an intricate design of
geometric and arabesque motifs. The Fatimid dynasty, which
claimed descent from the family of the prophet Muhammad, and
under whose patronage this manuscript was produced, ruled from
the 10th to the 12th century. Their empire stretched from Syria in
the East to the Atlantic coast of Morocco in the West.

**Rustam finds Kay Qubad, the Youthful Descendant
of Faridun, Enthroned on Mount Alburz**
Attributed to Aqa Mirak, Folio 110 from Shah Tahmasp's
Shahnama Tabriz, *c.* 1525-30
Miniature, 35.8 x 21.9cm (14 x 8½in); text, 26.7 x 21.9cm
(10½ x 8½in); page, 47 x 31.3cm (18½ x 12⅓in)
London, £793,500 ($1,198,185) 23.IV.96

The *Shahnama* or 'Book of Kings' is Persia's national epic, telling
the history and legends of the country from prehistoric times to
the seventh century AD. This version was made for Shah Tahmasp
at a time when the art of Persian painting had reached its zenith.
One of the supreme illustrated manuscripts of any period or culture,
it is among the greatest works of art in the world. This page broke
all records for any single leaf sold at auction.

**The Emperor Babur Celebrating the Birth
of His Son Humayun in the Char-bagh at Kabul in 1508**
Mughal, late 16th century
Tinted drawing on paper, margins ruled in green and gold,
gilt-decorated borders
27.3 x 14.6cm (10¾ x 5¾in)
New York, $52,900 (£34,914) 28.III.96

**An Illustration from the 'Isarda' *Bhagavata Purana*:
Yogamaya Manifested as a Girl Infant to the Dismay
of Kansa**
North India (Delhi Region), *c.* 1560
Yellow border with two lines of text on reverse
Folio, 19.1 x 26cm (7½ x 10¼in)
New York, $54,050 (£35,133) 21.IX.95

Humayun was Babur's first-born son and succeeded to the Mughal
throne in 1530. A version of this scene of celebration, by the artist
Sur Gujarati, is in the British Library's manuscript of the *Baburnama*.
This drawing was probably intended for inclusion in another manuscript copy of the *Baburnama* that describes the feast of Humayun's
nativity: 'All the bags, small and great brought gifts; such a mass
of white *tankas* was heaped up as had never been seen before. It was
a first-rate feast!'

As few as 20 pages survive from the *Bhagavata Purana* series, named
after Isarda, the place where it was discovered. The style is influenced
by early Mughal painting, suggesting that it dates from after the
establishment of the Mughal atelier and derives from the Delhi
region. This scene is from Chapter 4 of Book X, in which Krishna
is carried by Vasudeva across the Yamuna to safety after an exchange
of infants has flabbergasted his adversary, Kansa.

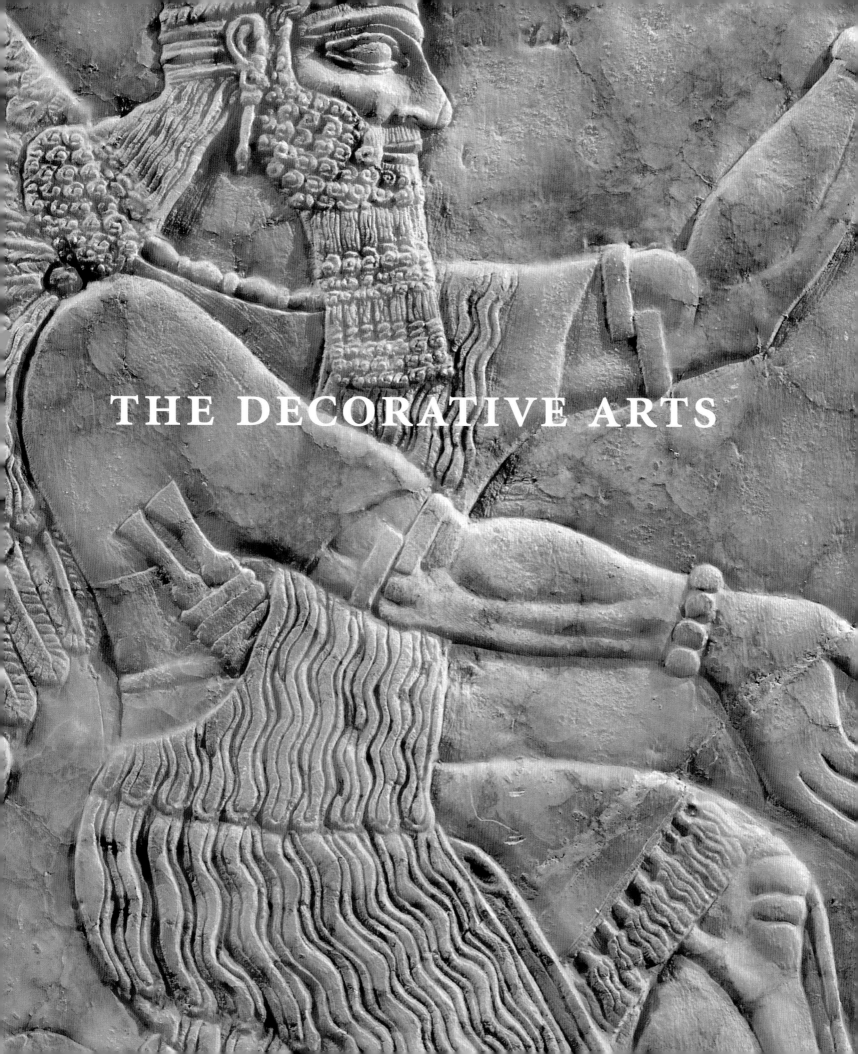

THE DECORATIVE ARTS

Islamic and Indian Art

A Hoysala Chloritic Schist Figure of an Elephant
Karnataka, *c.* 1200
Length, 66cm (26in)
London, £47,700 ($72,504) 25.IV.96

Elephant figures of this type were placed in pairs flanking the entrances to temple sancta. There are Hoysala examples in situ at the Panchikesvara temple, Halebid, and at the temple at Hariharapura. This work was discovered in a garden in Wales, where it had apparently languished for many years.

It is unusual to find medieval Hindu temple sculpture carved in the round, as here, most being executed in relief. The secular subject matter makes this piece broadly appealing, as does its naturalistic style.

A Kashan Lustre Pottery Dish

Persia, *c.* 1200
Rim diameter, 33cm (13in)
London, £78,500 ($119,320) 25.IV.96

The shallow-form dish is painted in brownish green on a cream ground with a scene depicting a long-haired falconer in an elaborate robe galloping through spiralling scrolls and leafy fronds. A bird is perched on the gauntlet of the rider's outstretched hand. Verses in Persian appear in a band of *sgraffiato* calligraphy around the rim. The painting on this piece shows all the features of an excellent example of the mature Kashan style.

A Hebrew-Inscribed Iznik Pottery Lamp

Turkey, *c.* 1575
Height, 25.6cm (10in)
London, £65,300 ($99,256) 25.IV.96

This unique hanging lamp is the only known example bearing a Hebrew inscription, indeed, it is the only piece of Iznik pottery to do so. Since the style links it to the later 16th century, one can only presume it was a private commission for the Jewish community in Turkey, almost certainly intended to adorn a synagogue in Istanbul. The piece has a flaring, trumpet-shaped neck and spherical body made in two parts. The overall pattern is of interlocking pointed medallions with symmetrical arabesque motifs.

Maqbool Fida Husain
Four Women, 1971
Signed in Hindi and dated
Acrylic on canvas, 1.52 x 1.51m (5ft x 5ft)
New York, $35,650 (£23,529) 3.IV.96
From the Chester and Davida Herwitz Charitable Trust

Maqbool Fida Husain, India's most famous artist, is essentially an expressionistic and symbolic painter. His celebratory use of colour can be seen in the vibrant hues with which he paints, while maintaining a simplicity of form. Fundamentally a humanist, Husain once said, 'Human beings, that's all that's really interesting. You paint and you draw in order to look at human beings ... to look at yourself'.

A Red Sandstone Figure of Shiva
Madhya Pradesh or Rajasthan, *c.* 10th century
Height, 124.5cm (49in)
New York, $85,000 (£56,100) 28.III.96

The contraposto stance of the divinity is the single most recognizable aesthetic trait that carries through much of medieval Indian stone sculpture. The fluid dancing pose found in both male and female figures connotes the liveliness and sensuous beauty that characterize the realm of the gods.

**A South Indian Bronze Figure of Shiva
as Lord of the Dance (*Nataraja*)**
Tamil Nadu Region, *c.* 14th century
Height, 70.5cm (27¾in)
New York, $151,000 (£98,150) 21.IX.95
*From the Mr and Mrs Klaus G. Perls Collection of Indian
and Southeast Asian Art*

The French sculptor Auguste Rodin was known to have seen bronzes from Southern India and to have admired the expertise in their casting. The icon of Shiva as Lord of the Dance is perhaps the most widely recognized subject represented in Hindu religious art, and this sculpture is particularly awe-inspiring for its delicate balance and exquisite detail.

Oriental Carpets and Rugs

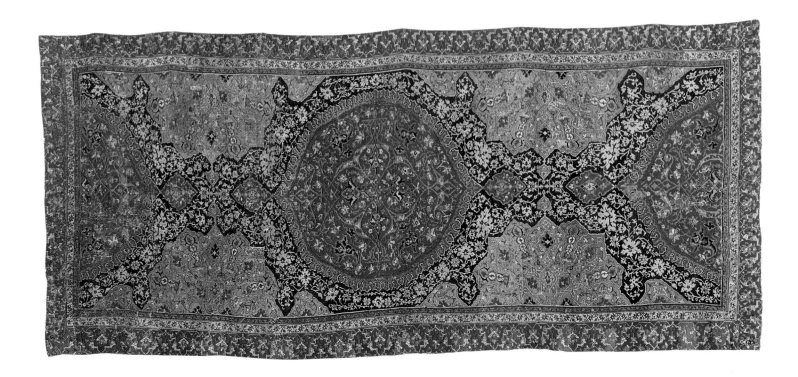

An Ushak Medallion Carpet
West Anatolia, late 16th century
5.45 x 2.40m (17ft 11in x 7ft 11in)
London, £89,500 ($136,040) 24.IV.96
From the Thyssen-Bentinck Collection

Known as the Cassirer Ushak Medallion, this carpet from the
collection of Baroness Gabrielle Thyssen-Bentinck is a rarity
among classical carpets. Previously in the collection of Baron
Heinrich Thyssen, it had not been seen on the market since the
1930s, when it was sold by Cassirer in Berlin. It was probably
created for court use as it is of the finest quality, beautifully
drawn, and its colours – ranging from ivory, yellow and pale
peach to deep red and walnut – are still vibrant.

A Mughal Millefleurs Prayer Rug
North India, first half of the 18th century
1.63 x 1.19m (5ft 4in x 3ft 11in)
New York, $805,500 (£531,630) 12.IV.96
From the Joseph R. Ritman Collection

Undoubtedly woven on commission for a wealthy, if not noble,
patron, this rug is one of a small group made during the late
17th and early 18th century under Mughul rule in India. Like
other pashmina-millefleurs rugs, it features the motif of a vase
issuing a multitude of flowering vines beneath an articulated
arch supported by cypress trees. The balance and intricacy of the
design, the use of pashmina wool and the fine execution indicate
that this is the product of a sophisticated workshop.

A Caucasian Carpet
18th century
3.07 x 1.50m (10ft 1in x 4ft 11in)
New York, $85,000 (£56,100) 12.IV.96

This rare example presents an amalgam of references to various 18th-century Caucasian weavings. The central motif of an eight-pointed star medallion with a central rosette surrounded by angular and stylized plant forms bears a striking resemblance to many 17th- and 18th-century Caucasian or Azerbaijan embroideries. Some aspects also recall early Caucasian dragon and floral carpets – geometric shapes framing the central medallion could be highly abstracted versions of dragons, and the vertical motifs bordering both sides of the field might reflect drop patterns of palmettes and rosettes.

An Azerbaijan Needlework Coverlet
17th century
1.95 x 1.48m (6ft 5in x 4ft 10in)
Bears the label '*International Exhibition of Persian Art, London, 1931, No. RA 7*'
London, £43,300 ($67,981) 18.x.95
From the Muncaster Castle Collection

This coverlet is from the collection of the Pennington family, who have been in residence at Muncaster Castle, Cumbria, since the 13th century. It is extremely rare due to its large size and its unique design, which does not feature a centralized medallion. A progression of ivory medallions contrasts with a field of flame-edged leaves that is reminiscent of the animal combats of the 17th-century Caucasian floral and dragon carpets.

Chinese Art

Lin Zihuan
Song of Ode
14th century, Yuan Dynasty
Ink on paper hand scroll
Jade clasp with carving of painter's name
and title of painting
26cm x 5.98m (10¼in x 19ft 7½in)
New York, $332,500 (£216,125) 18.IX.95

This hand scroll is one of two extant works
known by this artist. It retains its original
Qian Long imperial mounting and the label
and front title are written by the Emperor
himself. The Song of Ode is based on the
Southern Song composition by Ma Hezhi.
In this work Lin Zihuan took a new approach
in textual arrangement, and the brushstroke
quality exhibits the transition from naturalistic to more calligraphic styles that emerged
during the Yuan Dynasty.

Chang Yu (Sanyu)
White Lotus, *c.* **1930s**
Oil on canvas; signed *'yu'* in Chinese
in a square and *'SANYU'* in French
195 x 97cm (76¾ x 38¼in)
Taipei, NT$13,250,000 (£334,890; $523,265)
15.X.95

Despite Sanyu's early departure for France,
most of his works manifested his deeply
rooted Chinese origins. This painting is
another distinctive example of his Eastern
spirit, the white lotus being intimately associated with Buddhist iconography in Chinese
culture. According to legend, all lotus flowers
bloomed in celebration of the birth of the
Buddha. The flower is also considered divine
for its 'four virtues': fragrance, cleanliness,
loveliness and tenderness.

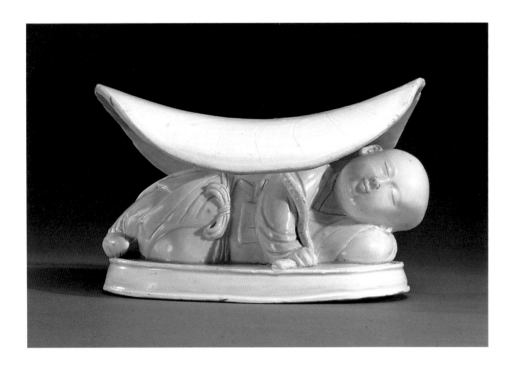

A Dingyao Pillow
Song Dynasty
Length, 20cm (8in)
New York, $134,500 (£86,080) 23.ix.95

Pillows such as this one in the form of a
plump little boy holding a lotus leaf are
mentioned by the late Ming writer Gao Lian
in the *Cunsheng bajian* ('Eight Discourses
on the Art of Living'), 1591. However, they
are extremely rare. Another example, now in
The Metropolitan Museum of Art, New York,
is incomplete and lacking its lotus leaf.

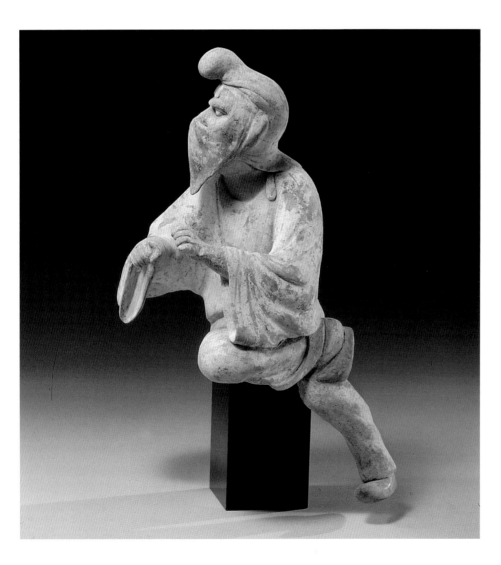

**Painted Pottery Figure
of a Masked Foreigner**
Tang Dynasty
Height, 30.5cm (12in)
New York, $112,500 (£74,250) 27.iii.96

This well-modelled figure realistically depicts a
mounted rider. With one leg crossed and one
extended as if riding side-saddle, and with
crooked arms raised, he appears to be holding
reins in his clenched fists. His powerful Persian
features peer over a pointed leather mask that
is dramatically pulled over the prominent nose.
The skin-coloured pigments also contribute
to the realism of the figure.

Jadeite Bangle

Interior diameter, approximately 5.3cm (2in);
thickness, 9.4mm (²⁄₅in)
Hong Kong, нк$9,920,000
(£813,114; $1,282,979) 1.xi.95

Bangles are symbols of good luck and are
traditionally given to the bride in Chinese
weddings. This magnificent jadeite piece is
highly translucent and of a brilliant green
colour throughout. Jadeite, structurally
different from nephrite, has been used for
Chinese jewellery since the 18th century.

Peking Enamel European-Subject Snuff Bottle

Mark and period of Qianlong (1736–95)
Height, 4.6cm (1⁴⁄₅in)
Hong Kong, нк$460,000 (£39,660; $59,195)
2.v.96

During the 18th century, due to the presence
of the Jesuit Fathers at the Imperial Court,
there was a fashion for all things European.
This snuff bottle is delicately painted on each
side with a heart-shaped panel containing a
European maiden in a landscape. On one side
she is depicted holding a flower and cradling
more blooms in her skirt, on the other she
carries a platter of fruit, and a European
village is visible in the distance.

A Wucai Inkstone
Mark and period of Wanli (1573–1619),
Ming Dynasty
21.5cm (8½in)
London, £298,500 ($456,705) 11.VI.96

It is very rare to find inkstones of this
elaborate design and only four others, all
museum pieces, are recorded. This particular
example is made of thick porcelain, pierced
and decorated in relief with dragons pursuing
pearls. *Wucai* (literally, 'five colours') is a
term for the application of vibrant enamels
to white porcelain, sometimes already under-
glazed in blue. The technique was developed
in the reign of Xuande (1426–35) and
perfected in the reign of Chenghua (1465–87).

A Purple-Splashed Junyao Basin
13th century, Jin/Yuan Dynasty
32.4cm (12¾in)
Hong Kong, HK$6,070,000 (£497,540;
$785,049) 31.X.95

This basin is one of the largest pieces of
splashed Jun ware known, as well as one
of the most striking. The only other vessel
of this type to be recorded is the famous
piece excavated in 1955 at Donguan, near
Baoding, in Hebei province, which is now
in the Hebei Provincial Museum. Although
larger in size, that piece is splashed in a less
vivid fashion than this example.

A Blue and White Lobed Basin

Mark and period of Wanli (1573–1619),
Ming Dynasty
37cm (14½in)
Hong Kong, HK$1,200,000 (£98,360; $155,199) 31.x.95

This eight-foliate lobed basin was made in the reign of the Emperor Wanli, the last important period of the Ming Dynasty. It is decorated with images of a scholar seated on a stool being attended by his servant in a garden landscape. The underglaze blue is of a deep inky tone. No other blue-and-white basin of this attractive design appears to be recorded, although there is a closely related piece with a different figure subject in Peking.

Korean Art

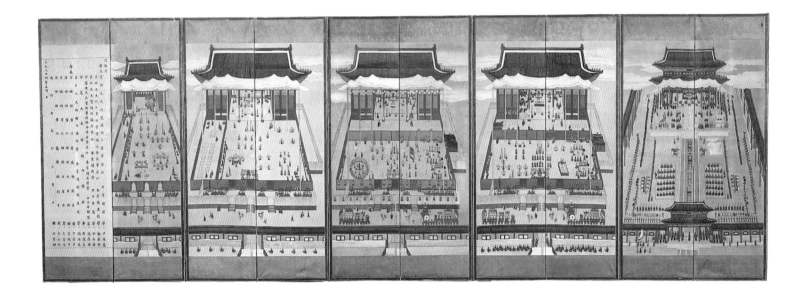

Ten-panel screen
19th century, with inscription on far left panel
Ink and colours on silk, mounted on brocade
1.82 x 5.11m (6ft x 16ft 9¼in)
New York, $1,157,500 (£763,950) 27.III.96

This newly discovered, monumental painting commemorates
the *chin'an*, the royal banquet held to celebrate the 80th
Birthday of Queen Mother Cho in 1887. Born in 1808, the
Queen Mother was a member of one of the most influential
clans of the latter part of the Chosen period. Feasts such as
these were not mere entertainment, but rituals, heavily imbued
with Confucian ideologies. Reflecting the strict philosophy
adopted by the scholars of the period, the paintings were
executed in an archaic, non-personal style.

Japanese Art

Egrets in a Marsh
Sesshu School (16th Century)
Pair of six-fold screens; ink and slight colour
on paper, mounted on brocade; each screen
approximately 1.47 x 3.57m
(4ft 10in x 11ft 8½in)
New York, $387,500 (£255,750) 29.111.96

These screens appear to be the work of a
follower of the great Muromachi painter
Sesshu (1420–1506). Although they are neither
signed nor sealed, the brushwork suggests
that the painter was well acquainted with
Sesshu's distinctive depictions of birds
in landscapes.

An Inlaid Iron Dish
By Shoan Katsuyoshi
Meiji period (1869–1912); signed *'Tokyo
ju Shoan Katsutoshi'*
41.3cm (16¼in)
London, £25,300 ($39,215) 19.VI.96

Decorated with high relief copper, gilt and
silver, this dish is a very good example of the
extremely fine metalwork produced during
the late 19th century, most notably by the
Komai factory. In this case, the maker was
Shoan Katsuyoshi, who worked for Miyao
and Co. in Tokyo during that period.

A Large Group of Two Dragons
18th century
10.5cm (4½in)
London, £43,300 ($67,548) 17.XI.95

This *netsuke*, or toggle, made of wood with a
rich patina, is unusually large. The subject –
two dragons standing on their tails in
heraldic form, holding a partially pierced ball
– is also extremely rare. Only one similar
piece appears to be recorded.

Ko-Imari Jar in Kakiemon Style
Second half of 17th century
London, £106,000 ($165,360) 17.XI.95

Imari was the European name for porcelain made for export at Arita and shipped from the port of Imari from the late 17th century onwards. This rare jar is decorated in the style of Sakaida Kakiemon, one of the most famous Japanese porcelain makers and painters, credited with the introduction into Japan, in 1644, of the process of painting in overglaze enamel colours.

An Early Nabeshima Dish
Late 17th century; 20cm (7⅞in)
Amsterdam, DFL401,000 (£155,758; $234,338)
21.V.96

In 1660 a Korean potter Ri Sampei discovered a source of kaolin near Arita and moved an entire village of craftsmen there. Much of the finest Japanese porcelain was made in kilns at Okachia or Okawachi near Arita, which were exclusively patronized by members of the local noble family, Nabeshima. These were mainly boldly painted plates, some-times decorated with rich interlaced designs recalling those on silk kimonos. The textile pattern on this rare, early example seems to be unrecorded.

Taiheiki ('Record of Peace')
17th century
Hand scroll with 16 illustrations in ink,
colour and gold on paper interspersed
with calligraphy text
33cm x 15.21m (1ft 1in x 49ft 10¾in)
New York, $294,000 (£191,100) 19.IX.95

The *Taiheiki* ('Record of Peace') recounts the
struggle between the Kyoto Imperial Court
and the *bakufu* (military feudal government)
during the time of the Southern and
Northern Courts (1334–1390). Covering a
period of over 50 years, it is a complex story
of countless battles in a brutal civil war.
This scroll belongs to the earliest known set
of Taiheiki hand scrolls which dates from
the 17th century and, most likely, consisted
originally of 12 scrolls.

**Shinshinto Katana, mei Minamoto
Masayuki [Kiyomaro]**
dated Tempo 15 (1844)
Nagasa (blade length) 81.5cm
New York, $288,500 (£187,525) 19.IX.95

This Japanese *katana* or 'long sword' is a
rare example by one of the finest sword-
smiths of the 19th century. Yamaura Tamaki
(1813–1854), known as 'Kiyomaro', was born
in Shinshu Province and learned the art of
sword-making from his older brother.

Kiyomaro's swords are technically masterful
and reflect the dynamism characteristic of
blades made during the tumultuous age when
Japan was opening up to the West. Kiyomaro
killed himself at the age of 42.

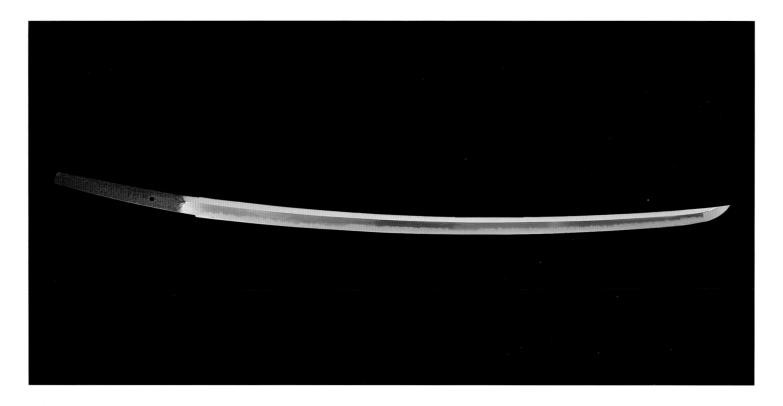

Tribal Art

A Fang Reliquary Guardian Head
Height, 40cm (15¾in)
New York, $783,500 (£517,110) 8.v.96

Fang sculpture has always been one of the most admired and sought after genres of African art. Helena Rubenstein was amongst the best known collectors of this type of art and the first to have this magnificent head in her collection. Reliquary guardian heads were rarer than the full-scale figures in Gabon, Equatorial Guinea and the Cameroons. This is one of the few unequivocally male Fang heads. It is more than likely that the trace of a beard denotes power and virility.

An Austral/Society Islands Flywhisk Handle
20cm (7⅞in)
New York, $107,000 (£70,620) 8.v.96

In earlier centuries, these Polynesian janus flywhisks were thought to originate from the island of Tahiti. More recent analysis, based on the records of museums, the journals of the men who collected the whisks, and the logs of the ships that carried them, has broadened the geographical location to the Society, Austral or Cook Islands. The distinct, deeply grooved, vertical rows of repeating chevrons on the slender, fluted handle often appear on this type of whisk. The janus figures are particularly elegant.

A Cook Islands, Raratonga Head of a Staff God
61cm (24in)
New York, $530,500 (£339,520) 14.XI.95
Property from the Collection of Joanne Coffin Clark

The appearance of this new Raratonga Islands staff god head was a major event. These sacred sculptures are amongst the rarest from all of Polynesia. Raratongan artists were master woodworkers, carving intricate openwork from hard casurina wood using stones and/or shells. The 20 known staff gods were executed in varying lengths, up to 13 feet long. Unlike most, which were collected by British missionaries, this one came into the hands of a New England whaler, though its exact provenance remains unclear.

Pre-Columbian Art

A Large Tolima Gold Figural Pendant

c. AD 500–1000

Height, 22.5cm (8⅞in)

New York, $288,500 (£187,525) 20.XII.95

From the Collection of Laurence C. Witten II

This boldly stylized figure, cast and hammered with symmetrically balanced splayed arms and legs, is perhaps only one of two or three known examples of such size. Tolima abstract anthropomorphic figures usually appear as either winged bodies, or, like this piece, with opposed limbs. Produced by lost-wax casting, these highly geometric pendants are remarkable for the equality of their parts – arms and legs always have the same length and no anatomical details ever appear.

A Colima Face Mask
Protoclassic, *c.* 100 BC – AD 250
Height, 20.3cm (8in)
New York, $82,250 (£54,285) 14.V.96

The region of western Mexico was home to the Protoclassic cultures of Colima, Nayarit and Jalisco. Colima ceramics display a wide variety of subjects and forms and are noted for their naturalistic style. This life-size mask is unusual for its idealized portraiture, an almost perfect oval facial plane, with a slight smile and aquiline nose. Though masks in this area may have been used for funerary purposes, some continue to be employed in shamanic rituals and this one may have served a ceremonial function.

American Indian Art

A Plateau Man's Beaded and Fringed Hide War Shirt
Width across the arms, 1.66m (5ft 5½in)
New York, $200,500 (£132,330) 21.v.96
Property from a Northeastern Educational Institution

This war shirt, made prior to 1860, was once in the collection of
Captain George Emerson Albee of the U.S. Infantry. Albee played a
prominent role in the Indian Wars. Consisting of finely tanned hide,
tiny glass beads and hair pendants, it is an excellent example of a
pre-Reservation period work. Such objects are rarely seen at auction,
having been acquired early and placed in museum collections.

**A Haida Chief's Ceremonial Dance
Headdress**
Height of frontlet, 17.8cm (7in)
Total height, 41.3cm (16¼in)
New York, $68,500 (£44,525) 30.XI.95

Made by native people of the Northwest
Coast, this headdress comprises an elaborate
wood frontlet and printed cotton cloth
headpiece wrapped on a metal wire. The
frontlet, or forehead mask, is in high relief
with a totemic crest animal, possibly a grizzly
bear, which has a delicately carved frog
perched on its abdomen. The use of abalone
shell and sea lion's whiskers highlights this
culture's relationship with the sea. This piece
boasted a fine provenance, much of which
was written on small labels that remain on
the interior.

Antiquities

**An Assyrian Gypsum Relief Fragment from Room I
of the North-west Palace of Assurnasirpal II at Nimrud**

Reign of Assurnasirpal II, 885–856BC

78.7 x 90.2cm (31 x 35½in)

New York, $5,667,500 (£3,683,875) 8.XII.95

Property from the Mr and Mrs Klaus G. Perls Collection of Antiquities

This relief fragment is one of the many that lined the walls of the Palace of Assurnasirpal II at Nimrud, which was excavated by Austen Henry Layard from 1845–48. The relief's transcendent aura of both majesty and might combined with its magnificent condition make it one of the finest examples of Ancient Near Eastern Art to have come on the market in recent years. The price achieved is a record for any antiquity at auction in the United States.

An Egyptian Life-size Bronze Figure of a Cat

Late Period, 26th Dynasty, *c.* 664–525BC
Height, 38cm (15in) without tang;
43cm (17in) with tang
London, £238,000 ($371,280) 2.VII.96

The cat was important in ancient Egypt both as a pet and as a sacred symbol of the goddess Bastet. Many places for the worship of Bastet existed throughout Egypt, the most important being at Bubastis (modern Tell Basta in the eastern Nile Delta), where a large cat cemetery and temple were discovered and where a quantity of bronze cats were found. This example is particularly impressive because of its size – the largest Egyptian cat in the British Museum, the 'Gayer-Anderson' cat, also measures 38cm.

An Egyptian Black Granite Kneeling Statue of King Amenhotep II

New Kingdom, 18th Dynasty, *c.* 1426–1400BC
Height, 71.1cm (28in); width, 30.5cm (12in);
depth, 36.9cm (14½in)
London, £419,500 ($641,835) 14.XII.95
From the Castle Howard Collection

Egypt became the greatest empire of its day during the New Kingdom (*c.*1550–1163BC) and was the dominant power over much of the Ancient Near East. King Amenhotep II (*c.* 1426–1400BC) played an active role in achieving this. Unusually tall and strong for an Egyptian king, he is depicted here holding two *nu* pots as an offering to the gods. This figure comes from the renowned collection formed by the 4th and 5th Earls of Carlisle in the 18th century.

Egyptian Bronze Head of a King or God
22nd Dynasty, probably reign of
Sheshonk I/Osorkon I, 944–888 BC
Height, 9.5cm (3¾in)
New York, $266,500 (£173,225) 13.VI.96

Cast for attachment to a large figure in
bronze or another media, this head's idealized
features and serene expression are inspired by
works from the 18th Dynasty and represent,
on a small scale, the art of ancient Egypt at
its finest. In 1977, it was sold at Sotheby Parke
Bernet, New York, by Greta S. Heckett and
was exhibited in Pittsburgh in the 1960s
at the Carnegie Institute's special exhibition
of Mrs Heckett's collection of ancient art.

Garden Statuary

**One of a Pair of Limestone Female Figures
on Rectangular Pedestals**
19th century
Height, 1.98m (6ft 6in); width, 99.1cm (3ft 3in)
New York, $28,750 (£18,687) 27.VI.96

Each of these seated female figures holds a cornucopia and rests near
a dolphin, emblems that represent earth and sea. The rectangular
base is carved with putti flanking a cabochon surmounted by ram
masks and birds.

Mark H. Blanchard
After the Antique: a Terracotta Figure of the Capitoline Flora
1889, square base stamped '*M. H. BLANCHARD, TERRACOTTA,
BLACKFRIARS RD LONDON 1889*'
Height, 1.57m (5ft 2in)
Square pedestal height, 54cm (29¼in)
Sussex, £21,850 ($32,994) 21.V.96

This figure is based on a statue bought by the Pope in 1744 and
placed in the Capitoline Museum. The director of the French
Academy in Rome, Jean François de Troy, wrote that it was 'one of
the most beautiful draped figures in the whole of Rome'. Mark
Blanchard served his apprenticeship with Coade and Sealy, setting up
his own works in 1839. Although he later used a more fashionable,
strongly coloured terracotta, some of Blanchard's earlier pieces are
indistinguishable from Coade's.

European Works of Art

**A Fine Boxwood Figure
of the Dancing Venus**
Nuremberg, early 16th century
Height, 29.3cm (11½in)
on a material-covered base
London, £287,500 ($448,500) 4.VII.96
*From the Collection Formed by the British
Rail Pension Fund*

This renowned boxwood figure of the
Dancing Venus has been well documented,
yet no satisfactory attribution has been
agreed upon. However, it is clear that the
drawings of Albrecht Dürer were a main
source of inspiration, particularly his engraving of the *Women's Bath*. In that work,
a naked bather, also elongated in shape,
stands in a similar pose, with one arm raised
and the other down by her side. This piece
was formerly on view in the Victoria and
Albert Museum, London.

**A Netherlandish Bronze 'Aeolipile'
or Steamblower**
c. 1580–1600
Height, 40cm (15¾in)
New York, $475,500 (£304,320) 9.1.96
*From the Private Collection and Gallery
of the Blumka Estate*

The *aeolipile* was used in antiquity to
blow steam onto a burning fire. Named
after Aeolus, the Greek god of the winds,
these objects were a source of entertainment
in the 15th and 16th centuries. During the
Renaissance sphinxes were commonly associated with fire and death and often decorated
chimneys, andirons and candelabra. This
highly imaginative example features a bejewelled sphinx, with puffed cheeks and lips
pursed to blow air, perched on a grinning
satyr that gnaws the wings of a pelican.

**A French Ivory Relief Panel from a Casket
with Scenes from the Hunt**

Paris, c. 1330–1350
10.6 x 24.8cm (4¼ x 9¾in)
New York, $107,000 (£69,550) 14.VI.96

The first three of the four compartments comprising this panel are
carved with scenes of lovers on horseback. Some hold falcons, while
one figure blows a horn. The fourth compartment shows people
before a castle. Although the hunt was a common subject in the art
of the Gothic period, ivory objects incorporating secular images
were much more rare than those with religious themes.

**A Roman Gilt Bronze Presentation Model
for the Seal of Cardinal Giulio de' Medici, attributed
to Lautizio da Perugia, c. 1513**

Height, 11.7cm (4⅝in)
New York, $261,000 (£169,650) 14.VI.96

This gilt relief has been accepted as the presentation model from
which the intaglio seal was made for Cardinal Giulio de'Medici,
Pope Clement VII (1523–34). It has been skilfully worked with the
Madonna kneeling in the foreground before the Christ Child. Saint
Peter is standing behind her on the right, Saint Paul to the left and
Saint Lawrence in the centre. Below, two angels uphold a cardinal's
hat from which a shield with the Medici arms is suspended.

A White Marble Bust of 'a Man in a Hat' Attributed to Giuste le Court

Venetian, 1627–1678
Height, 72.5cm (28in)
Marble socle and tapering marble pedestal,
1.10m (3ft 7½in) high
London, £205,000 ($315,700) 7.XII.95

Giuste le Court was born in Ypres and as a young man carved a Madonna for the cathedral at Antwerp. He later worked in Padua on the tomb of Catherina Cornaro in the Santo. Most of his work is religious and this bust, with its distinctive pilgrim's hat, may be an interpretation of St Roch. It can also be compared with the figure of St Mark on the high altar of the Salute church in Venice, a city in which the artist lived for a time.

19th-Century Sculpture

Vittorio Caradossi
Shooting Stars
Marble, inscribed '*Prof. V. Caradossi Firenze*'
Height, 1.82m (6ft)
New York, $387,500 (£244,125) 1.XI.95

Caradossi (Italian, b. 1861) specialized
in creating celestial and ethereal maidens
in compositions such as this *chef d'oeuvre*
depicting two female personifications of
shooting stars spiralling upwards. His other
works include *Tre Nereidi* ('Three Mermaids')
and *Il Fumo che Sale Verso le Nubi* ('Smoke
Sweeping up to the Clouds'), the latter
of which was exhibited at the Paris Salon
des Artistes Français in 1909. Here, the two
sinuous, intertwined figures carved out of a
single block of marble uniquely demonstrate
the artist's technical virtuosity.

Sir Alfred Gilbert
Eros
Aluminium, modulated black patina over
natural aluminium silver colour;
bronze base
Figure height, 2.90m (9ft 6in);
width, 1.92m (6ft 3½in);
wingspan, 1.13m (3ft 9in);
base height, 2.37m (7ft 10in)
London, £199,500 ($301,245) 22.V.96

Sir Alfred Gilbert's *Eros* is to London what
the Eiffel Tower is to Paris or the Statue
of Liberty is to New York. In 1987 a limited
edition of casts was taken from Gilbert's
original plasters of the 19th-century *Eros*,
following the statue's removal from
Piccadilly Circus for restoration and exhibition. These were done under the direction
of George Mancini, who had worked with
Gilbert on his lost-wax castings. Ten casts
were made for the 1987 edition, of which
seven are in private ownership.

English Furniture

Pair of George III Giltwood Open Armchairs
c. 1760
New York, $178,500 (£117,810) 12.IV.96

These important chairs feature cartouche-shaped backrests surmounted by a pierced cresting carved with a cabochon and foliage. The scrolled armrests, apron and feet closely relate to a design by Thomas Chippendale for 'French Chairs' illustrated in *The Gentleman and Cabinet-Maker's Director*, 1754.

**Pair of George III Carved Mahogany Armchairs
Attributed to William Vile**

c. 1760
London, £837,500 ($1,306,500) 5.VII.96

These armchairs form part of an extensive suite originally commissioned by the 4th Earl of Shaftsbury for St Giles's House, Dorset. They were probably made by the royal cabinet-maker William Vile, who worked extensively for George III.

**Pair of George III Satinwood Secretaire Cabinets
Attributed to Chippendale, Haig & Co.**
Third quarter 18th century
Height, 2.27m (7ft 5½in); width, 1.25m (4ft 1in);
depth, 58.4cm (23in)
New York, $321,500 (£212,190) 12.IV.96

Chippendale, Haig & Co. was formed in 1771 by Thomas
Chippendale, Thomas Haig and Henry Ferguson. Thomas
Chippendale the Younger continued the association with Haig
after his father's death in 1779. This pair of secretaire cabinets has
marked sylistic affinities with other examples of furniture associated
with the firm.

George II Carved Marble Chimney-Piece Attributed to Sir Henry Cheere

c. 1755
London, £188,500 ($297,830) 10.XI.96

Carved in Carrara marble overlaying Siena marble and Sicilian jasper, this chimney-piece is among the masterpieces of English Rococo, a work that challenges the boundaries between the fine and decorative arts. Carved in only three sections and in high relief, it contains an abundance of naturalistic ornament, including birds, squirrels, trailing foliage, floral festoons, cascading water and shellwork. It was almost certainly made by Sir Henry Cheere (1703–81), a leading figure in 18th-century sculpture and design.

George III Chinese Mirror Painting

c. 1760
Height, 2.8m (6ft 9¾in);
width, 11.8m (3ft 10½in)
London £298,500 ($471,630) 10.XI.96

This important mirror painting is among the largest recorded examples of its kind and achieved a world-record price at auction. It was formerly in the collection of Sir James Horlick, 4th Baronet (1886–1958), a noted connoisseur and collector who assembled a particularly important group of 18th-century Chinoiserie furniture.

19th-Century Furniture

**A Pair of French Gilt-bronze and Lapis Lazuli
Side Tables, signed by Henri Dasson**
Paris, dated 1878 and 1880 respectively
77.5 x 93.5 x 54cm (30½ x 36¾ x 21¼in)
London, £62,000 ($97,960) 6.x.95

One of these tables, topped with lapis lazuli and rouge marble, is
decorated with emblems of the liberal arts. The other, of *verde antico*
marble, displays the attributes of the seasons. Henri Dasson was
an important Parisian furniture-maker who made many copies
of 18th-century models, often in the style of Louis XVI. His gilt-
bronze decorations are particularly striking. Unusually, the friezes
embellishing these tables have been laid onto a lapis ground, which
emphasizes their exceptionally rich quality.

**A Kingwood Marquetry and Gilt-bronze Side Cabinet,
by Frédéric Schmit**

c. 1900; labelled *'Schmit Ebenisterie d'Art Tapisserie,
22 rue d'Charnonne'* with stencilled number *'5006'*
139 x 155 x 54cm (54¾ x 61 x 21¼ in)
London, £52,100 ($78,671) 24.v.96

This extraordinary, marble-topped side cabinet features sculptural
bronze reliefs of a scantily clad water nymph and swags of flowers
and shells flanked by dolphins. Eighteenth-century French styles
are combined with marquetry landscapes deriving from Japanese
woodcuts. It is a fine example of the imaginative furniture produced
in the Paris workshop of Frédéric Schmit. In the second half of
the 19th century he was generating his best work and received gold
medals at the Expositions Universelles in 1878 and 1889.

Napoleon III Style Mahogany Jardinière

Third quarter 19th century. 99.1 x 108cm (39 x 42½in)
New York, $39,100 (£25,415) 6.III.96

This gilt-bronze and porcelain-mounted jardinière features a
pierced gallery and trestle-form mounts enclosing flower heads.
The garden theme is extended to the inset floral and figural plaques.

A Louis XIV Style Fire Screen, by Alfred Beuderley

Late 19th century; fitted with Wedgwood plaques, stamped *'BY'*
104cm x 69.9cm (41in x 27½in). New York, $34,500 (£22,425), 6.III.96
Property from the Estate of Marion Blacklock Miller

A successful Parisian furniture-maker, Alfred Beuderley specialized
in copies of 18th-century originals. This firescreen is in the manner
of Pierre Gouthière, whose works were much imitated. The caryatids
and scrolling rose branches are typical of his neoclassical style.

American Decorative Arts

Samuel Whitehorne Queen Anne Block-and-Shell-Carved Mahogany Kneehole Desk, Attributed to Edmund Townsend
Newport, Rhode Island, *c.* 1780
83.8 x 92.1 x 52.1cm (33 x 36¼ x 20½in)
New York, $3,632,500 (£2,397,450) 20.1.96
From the Collection of Mr & Mrs Adolph Henry Meyer

The only known example of this rare form that has survived with its original finish, this desk remains in untouched condition. Its attribution to Edmund Townsend is based on comparisons with a similar, labelled desk in the Museum of Fine Arts, Boston. A prominent citizen in Newport, Rhode Island, Townsend was a highly individual cabinet-maker. The graceful elegance of this piece, the shells and ogee feet, are characteristic of his furniture. Its first owner was Samuel Whitehorne, a prosperous Newport merchant and distiller.

**Edward Jackson Parcel-gilt Inlaid and
Figured Mahogany Mirrored Bonnet-top
Secretary Bookcase**
Boston, Massachusetts, 1738–48
Two inked inscriptions on paper labels
2.34m x 1.01m x 64.8cm
(7ft 8in x 3ft 3¼in x 25½in)
New York, $1,432,500 (£945,450) 20.1.96
*From the Collection of Mr & Mrs Adolph
Henry Meyer*

This superlative desk and bookcase is part
of a group of furniture made in Boston that
represents a highly sophisticated tradition
combining the efforts of several talented
artisans. These pieces reflect an intimate
understanding of late seventeenth-century
Baroque, Palladian Classicism and the
furniture traditions of eighteenth-century
Boston. The designer is unknown, but had
apparently absorbed both Bostonian and
British styles. Owned by Edward Jackson, a
member of one of Boston's leading families,
the desk was passed down through
several generations.

A Canvaswork Chimney-piece, by Schoolgirl Hannah Otis (1732–1801)
Boston, Massachusetts, *c.* 1750
Wool, silk, metallic threads and beads on linen
62.2 x 132.7cm (24½ x 52¼in)
New York, $1,157,500 (£763,950) 20.1.96
Property of the Otis Family

This magnificent chimney-piece was made by a teenage girl while studying at a Boston boarding school. Generally girls took their subjects from prints and patterns presented to them by their teachers, but Hannah Otis depicts her personal view of Boston – including her favourite landmarks, the Thomas Hancock House, the beacon on Beacon Hill, and her friends, John Hancock and his prominent family. The fort on the left, flying the King's flag, refers to the controversial presence of British soldiers in Boston at the time.

James Bard
Schooner Lewis R. Mackey, 1858
Signed and dated *'Picture Drawn & Painted by James Bard/162 Perry Street, NY, 1858, Dec'*
Oil on canvas, 78.7 x 132.7cm (31 x 52¼in)
New York, $255,500 (£166,075) 21.VI.96
Property of the Lee County Alliance of the Arts

This lot was accompanied by a letter by Anthony Peluso stating that the '*Lewis Mackey* probably carried bricks from up-Hudson River. The captain in this painting appears to be calling to the rower to retrieve his box which has fallen overboard. In front of the palisaded background is the Steam-boat *Radiant!* and the Sloop *Equal Rights!* Two other versions of this painting by Bard are known, one includes a lighthouse, the other porpoises.'

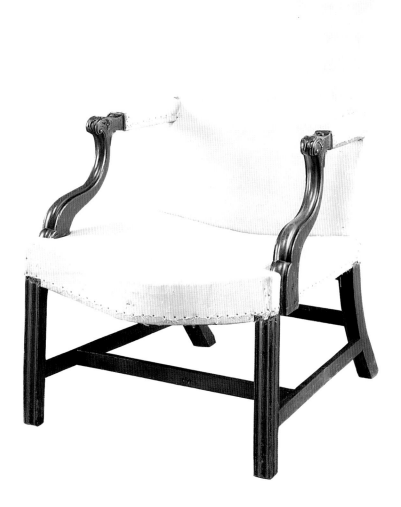

A Painted Pine Carving from the Packet Ship *Congress*
Depicting Liberty with Shield and Eagle
Maine, *c.* 1840
94cm (37in)
New York, $310,500 (£201,825) 21.VI.96
Property of the Estate of Loyal Farragut Sewall, Jr., Small Point, Maine

According to tradition, this decorative ship carving came from the packet ship *Congress*, which was built by S. Greenleaf in Pittston, Maine, up the Kennebec River from Bath. In his representation of Liberty, the woodcarver combines elements associated with mother Britannia and the feathered headdress of an Indian Princess. This iconic personification of America expressed the colonialists' loyalty to England as well as their more recent identity as citizens of the New World.

Joseph Wharton Chippendale Carved Mahogany
Upholstered Open Armchair
Philadelphia, Pennsylvania, *c.* 1770
Bears 19th-century brass plaque with engraved inscription,
'Chair of my Great Grandfather Joseph Wharton Chas. W. Wharton'
New York, $585,500 (£386,430) 20.I.96
From the Collection of Mr & Mrs Adolph Henry Meyer

The mate of this armchair is now in the White House. It is possible that it was made by Thomas Affleck, a leading Scottish cabinet-maker who immigrated to America in 1763, where he became an outstanding exponent of the American Chippendale style. The piece originally resided at Walnut Grove, the Philadelphia country estate of Joseph Wharton, venue of many fashionable social events in the late 1770s, including a fête honouring the departure of General Howe in 1778.

European Tapestries & Carpets

The Triumph of Galatea
Atelier of Guillaume Werniers,
after Antoine Coypel
Lille, *c.* 1730
3.50 x 4.60m (11ft 6in x 15ft)
London, £58,500 ($89,505) 29.11.96
From the Vigo-Sternberg Collection

The story of Acis and Galatea in Ovid's *Metamorphoses* is the inspiration for this tapestry from the Vigo-Sternberg collection of European Tapestries. The Cyclops Polyphemus falls passionately in love with the beautiful sea-nymph Galatea, but she rejects him for the handsome Acis. Finding them

together, Polyphemus crushes Acis with a rock. The sorrowful nymph then changes Acis into the river which flows at the foot of Mount Etna.

**Les Deux Taureaux, Gobelins Tapestry
from the series Les Nouvelles Indes,
after a Design by François Desportes
from the Le Blonde Atelier**
Dated 1753
Fully signed *'Desportes mp. xit.'*
and 'LeBlonde. ec. 1753'
4.26 x 4.93m (14ft x 16ft 2in)
New York, $321,500 (£205,760) 11.x.95
From the Ralph Lauren Collection

This tapestry forms part of a set woven after
cartoons by François Desportes called *Les
Nouvelles Indes*. The original designs upon
which Desportes based these cartoons were
by Albert Eckhout and were given to Louis
XIV by Prince Maurice de Nassau before 1693.
The weaving was owned by Ralph Lauren, the
renowned fashion designer. His remarkable
collection of English and Continental furniture and decorations embraces a diversity
of styles and cultures.

Continental Furniture

A Transitional Purplewood and Bur-Walnut Marquetry 'commode en bibliothèque'
Stamped *'Jean-François Oeben'*, c. 1763–68
92cm x 1.36m x 38cm (3ft x 4ft 5½in x 1ft 3in)
Monaco, FF7,068,500 (£883,563; $1,359,327) 15.VI.96
From the Collection of Mr and Mrs Delplace

Open-fronted commodes of this type, in the Louis XV style, are extremely rare. An identical piece, stamped 'J. H. Riesener' exists in Paris. This indicates that both were made between the end of Oeben's ownership of the workshop and the beginning of Riesener's. Oeben died in 1763 and his widow took charge of the cabinet-making business, still using her husband's stamp on furniture made by her employees, including Riesener, whom she married in 1767. Subsequently, he started to use his own name.

One of Eight German Boulle Marquetry and Tortoiseshell Chinoiserie Panels
Augsburg, early 18th century; 50 x 30cm (19¾ x 11¾in)
London, £782,500 ($1,197,225) 14.VI.96

The labels and crests appearing on this set of panels would suggest that they were commissioned in the period 1719–30 for the Schönborn family, one of the most important families in Germany at that time. Six of the episodes narrated on these panels relate to *The Story of the Emperor of China* (probably Kangxi, 1661–1721, and his wife). It is probable that they were conceived for the decoration of a particular room at the family's castle in Pommersfelden.

One of Two Matching Louis XV 'Vernis Martin' Red Lacquer Commodes
Stamped 'B.V.R.B'; c. 1755
84cm x 1.14m x 52cm (2ft 9in x 3ft 9in x 1ft 8½in)
Monaco, FF8,636,500 (£1,079,563; $1,660,578) 15.VI.96
From the Collection of the Duke de Doudeauville
and from the Late René Weiller

These commodes belong to a small group of five almost identical pieces
by B.V.R.B., one of which is in the Getty Museum, another in the Musée
of Dijon and a third in a collection in the west of France. Extremely rare,
they almost certainly correspond to five commodes known to have been
sold by the famous dealer Lazare Duvaux between 1754 and 1758 to
clients such as the Duke of Orléans, the Duchess of Mirepoix and the
Marquise of Haussy.

One of a Pair of German Rococo Ormolu-Mounted Fruitwood Marquetry Commodes
Mid-18th century; 85cm x 1.30m x 67cm
(2ft 9½in x 4ft 3½in x 2ft 2½in)
New York, $165,000 (£108,900) 18.v.96

This fine marquetry commode exhibits all the extravagance of the Rococo period. Raised on delicate cabriole legs, it is headed by ormolu chutes cast with foliage and a cabochon. The front is veneered with elaborate cartouches incorporating foliage and shell motifs enclosing mythological figures, floral sprays and birds. Each piece is topped with a piece of marble in a wonderful mottled yellow and ochre colour.

An Italian Kingwood and Tulipwood Marquetry Gueridon Table
Giuseppe Maggiolini, *c.* 1785; 70.5 x 35cm (24½ x 13¾in)
London, £199,500 ($305,235) 14.vi.96.

Giuseppe Maggiolini (1738–1814), one of the most talented 18th-century Italian *ebanisti*, was unsurpassed for the quality and inventiveness of his marquetry inlay. Very little is known about his life, and scant documentary evidence relating to his work survives. What makes the furniture of this Lombard cabinet-maker particularly notable is the use of up to 86 different woods to create marquetry pieces of outstanding quality and design, of which this is a very fine example.

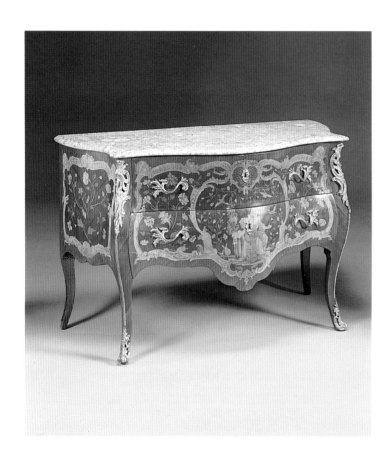

**A Louis XVI Ormolu-Mounted Mahogany
Bureau Plat and Cartonnier**
Etienne Levasseur, signed; 1.11m x 1.59m x 80.6cm
(3ft 7¾in x 5ft 2½in x 2ft 7¾in)
New York, $1,432,500 (£944,300) 24.IV.96
From the Estate of Jacqueline Kennedy Onassis

This *bureau plat* was amongst the highlights in the auction of articles
from the Jacqueline Kennedy Onassis Estate. Signed by Etienne
Lavasseur, it is known as 'The Nuclear Test Ban Table'. The middle
drawer is fitted with a brass plaque inscribed: *'DESK ON WHICH/
THE NUCLEAR TEST BAN TREATY/ WAS SIGNED BY/ PRESIDENT
JOHN FITZGERALD KENNEDY/ TREATY ROOM – THE WHITE
HOUSE/ AUGUST 5, 1963.'*

Ceramics & Glass

A Lambeth Delft Dish
c. 1720
29.2cm (11½in)
London, £45,500 ($69,160) 10.v.96

Part of the collection of Tristram Jellinek, this charming dish shows a naïve, stylized fox trotting gaily through a landscape of sponged trees in a green-washed clearing. 'Fox' was the maiden name of Jellinek's mother, and he collected many items featuring the animal. An actor with the Glasgow Citizen's Theatre, Tristram Jellinek died in 1995. He began his parallel career as an antiques dealer in the late 1960s with a stall in the Portobello Road, London, specializing in pottery. Eventually, he graduated to Lindsay Antiques, in Kensington Church Street.

A Meissen Two-Handled Pot-pourri Vase, Cover and Stand

c. 1880; crossed swords in blue underglaze, incised numerals and pressnummern
87cm (34¼in)
London, £10,350 ($16,146) 4.vi.96

During the 1880s when this vase was made, the Meissen factory was mainly producing versions of its earlier models, sometimes as direct copies, sometimes in embellished form. This vase is based on Meissen's 18th-century inverted pear shape, but lavishly decorated with a winged putto, a maiden, flowers, fruits and – unusually for a vase of this type – insects. It is finely painted on both sides with groups seated in Arcadian landscapes. The domed, pierced cover is topped with an elaborate floral finial.

The Sèvres Porcelain 'Service Decoration Riche en Couleurs et Riche en Or ... de la Reine' Marie Antoinette: the 'Service à Frise Riche'
Dated 1784
New York, $882,500 (£582,450) 18.v.96

This royal service was commissioned from the Sèvres factory by Marie Antoinette in 1784, but was diverted as a diplomatic gift from Louis XVI to King Gustave III of Sweden on the occasion of his visit to Paris that summer. Sèvres continued production for the Queen, however, and five years later made an identical service for her sister-in-law, the Comtesse d'Artois. This 300-piece service included items from all three sets, as well as 19th-century Herend porcelain supplements, and achieved one of the highest prices ever paid at auction for a porcelain service.

A Façon de Venise Diamond-Point Engraved Calligraphic Goblet

1688; signed under the foot, *'Willem van Heemskerk aes. 75. ao.1688, in Leiden'*
20.5cm (8⅛in)
London, £62,000 ($96,100) 14.XI.95

This goblet belonged to Joseph R. Ritman, who owned one of the world's finest collections of Dutch 16th- and 17th-century glass. Though the engraver Willem van Heemskerk worked as an amateur, he was amongst the foremost masters of his art. Such is the quality and rarity of his work that it is unusual to find examples outside museums. The funnel bowl of this piece is engraved in fine calligraphic script with the inscription: *Nemo sibi nascitur* ('We are not born for ourselves').

A Rare Longton Hall 'Strawberry Leaf' Soup Tureen and Cover

c. 1755
22.3 x 30.7cm (8¾ x 12⅛in)
New York, $17,250 (£11,385) 15.IV.96

Although other wares with this decoration are well known, this is the only 'Strawberry Leaf' tureen recorded. However, a piece of this octafoil shape, adorned with landscapes and a family crest and apparently made by William Littler, proprietor of the post-Longton Hall factory, during his later years at West Pans in Scotland, has recently come to light. It is evidence that he continued working with this important form a decade later. The interior of this example has been painted with two large tulips, sprigs of leaves and flowers, and a blue-winged insect.

A 'Pantin' Magnum Salamander Weight

19th century
10.8cm (4¼in)
New York, $68,500 (£44,525) 26.VI.96

This rare paperweight is a hitherto unrecorded example of the lizard/salamander type, of which there are apparently only twelve other existing examples. The coiled form of the reptile is faceted to reveal beige scales. Highly sought after for their characteristic three-dimensional designs and varied colour schemes, they are attributed to the French factory Pantin, about which very little is known. They have been described as the greatest technical achievements of 19th-century paperweight makers.

Applied Arts

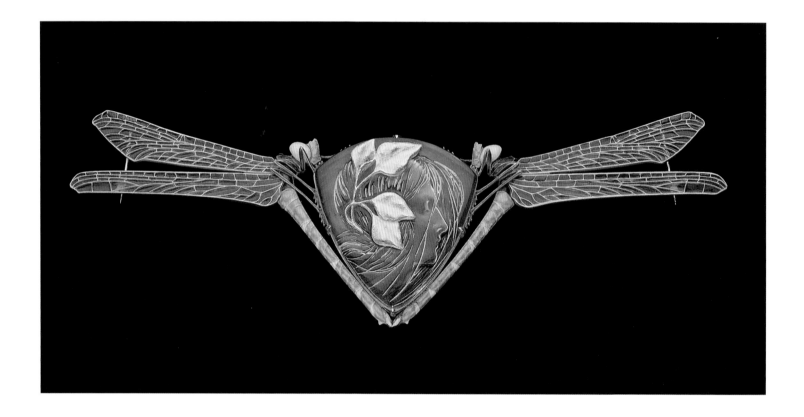

René Lalique
Water Nymph and Dragonfly Brooch/Cloak Clasp
1904–5; in original cream velvet and silk-lined brown leather
case; brooch stamped '*LALIQUE*', silk lining with gilt mark,
'*R LALIQUE/40 COURS-LA-REINE/PARIS*'
5 x 16.8cm (2 x 6⅝in)
Geneva sf218,500 (£123,446; $193,362) 16.xi.95

Lalique is legendary as a prolifically imaginative designer whose
great innovation was the highly inventive use of enamels and the
juxtaposition of precious and non-precious materials. His exquisite
creations were sought after by members of the fashionable world,
including the actress Sarah Bernhardt. This brooch is formed from
two dragonflies with bodies enamelled in transluscent pearly pink,
and hinged wings of *plique à jour*. They cling to a central triangle of
glass, intaglio-moulded with a profile of a nymph, her hair entwined
with gold leaves.

Charles Rennie Mackintosh
Chair for the Drawing Room, Hous'hill, Nitshill
Glasgow, 1904
75.5cm (29¾in)
London, £89,500 ($141,410) 3.11.96

This chair was made for the drawing room of Hous'hill, the Glasgow
home of Mackintosh's most important patron, Miss Cranston.
The subtle, curved rails echoed the slender, vertical ribs of the gently
bowed screen in front of which it was placed. A contemporary
photograph suggests that there was a central armchair with two pairs
of flanking chairs, of which this is one. Incorporating a decorative
oval of lilac glass, it is one of Mackintosh's most sophisticated,
elegant designs.

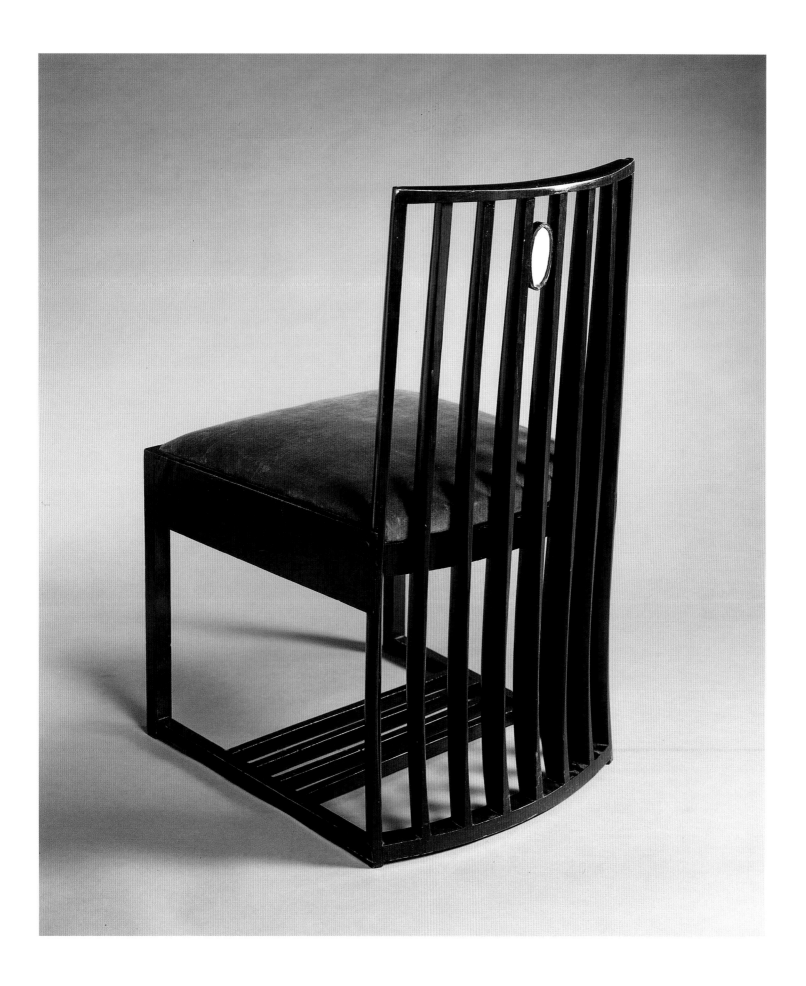

Louis Comfort Tiffany
A Fine Favrile Glass Landscape Window
c. 1900; 2.13 x 1.83m (7 x 6ft)
New York, $266,500 (£173,225) 5.vi.96
From the Warshawsky Corporate Collection

This large, arched window utilizes Tiffany's patented handmade glass, 'favrile', which was made iridescent by exposure when molten to the fumes of vaporized metals. It was manufactured for Carmore, the home of Charles Rushmore in Woodbury Falls, New York, and originally installed on the stair landing. Later, it came into the encyclopedic collection of Roy Warshawsky whose goal was to furnish his corporate offices with a wide selection of Tiffany objects.

Louis Comfort Tiffany
Favrile Glass and Bronze Filigree Poppy Lamp
1899–1920; shade impressed *'TIFFANY STUDIOS/NEW YORK/1581'*
base impressed 'TIFFANY STUDIOS/NEW YORK/10916'
66 x 50.8cm (26 x 20in)
New York, $151,000 (£98,150) 2.xii.95
From the Private Collection of Lloyd and Barbara Macklowe

The conical shade of this lamp is patterned with poppy blossoms in mottled opalescent glass overlaid with bronze filigree. It is from the collection of Lloyd and Barbara Macklowe, who were instrumental in bringing French Art Nouveau to America. They developed an interest in the style in the 1960s, opening their first gallery on Madison Avenue in the 1970s and eventually becoming the leading dealers of Art Nouveau and Art Deco in the United States.

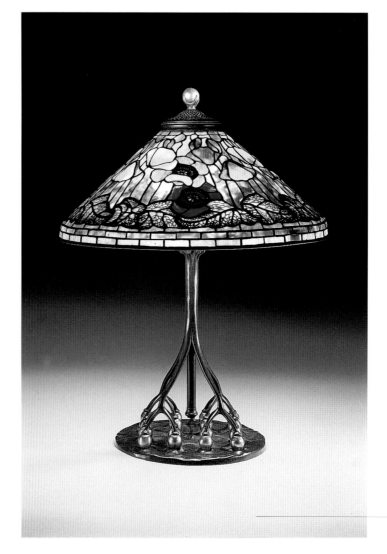

Da Silva Bruhns
Geometric Carpet
c. 1930; signed and monogrammed
Woven wool, 6.4 x 3.3m (20ft 2in x 10ft 1¾in)
London, £44,400 ($67,932) 29.III.96

Woven in shades of salmon pink wool, this stylish carpet was
commissioned by the Maharaja of Indore. He became a major patron
of contemporary design through his idea of furnishing his palace,
Manik Bagh, in the fashionable Modernist style. He ordered furniture
and furnishings from leading designers in Paris, including Eileen
Gray, Jacques-Emile Ruhlmann, Louis Sognot, Charlotte Alix and
Le Corbusier. All the carpets were created by da Silva Bruhns.

Marcel Coard
Table
c. 1929–30; 74.5 x 55cm (29⅓ x 21¾in)
Monaco, FF348,500 (£45,615; $69,979) 11.XII.95

This circular, three-layered table belonged to Paul and Marcelle
Cocteau. The brother of the French novelist, dramatist and draughtsman Jean Cocteau, Paul commissioned Coard to design the furniture
for his house in Touraine. Influenced by African and Oceanic art,
Coard's furniture made use of rare and unusual materials. He
favoured bold, emphatic forms and exploited rich, sometimes
contrasting materials, such as the red-brown lacquer and the
chequered squares of mother-of-pearl in this piece.

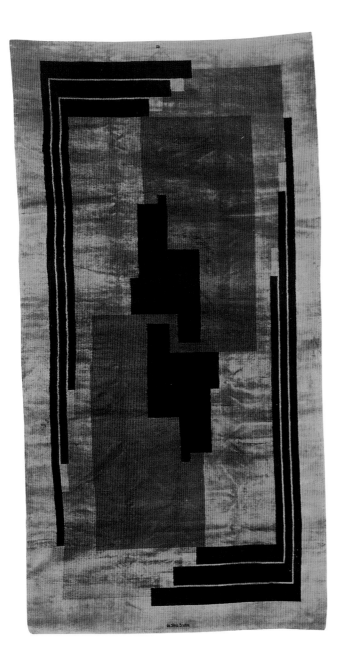

Jean Michel Frank
A Stained Beech and Galuchat-Veneered
Oak Commode executed by Adolphe Chanaux
1927; impressed, '*MADE IN FRANCE*' (three times), Chanaux cipher
88.3cm x 1.25m x 44.5cm (2ft 10¾in x 4ft 1in x 17½in)
New York, $332,500 (£216,125) 2.XII.95

One of the earliest known collaborative pieces by Jean Michel
Frank and Adolphe Chanaux, this extraordinary commode is
veneered in galuchat with a sunburst pattern. Above two curved,
panelled doors, the D-form top is flanked by swollen side panels.
The supports and tapering feet are of mahogany-stained beech.
Chanaux and Frank were introduced in 1927 and began a friendship
and collaboration that lasted until the latter's early death in 1941.
Prior to their association, Chanaux had worked with Jacques-Emile
Ruhlmann and André Groult.

Ernest Boiçeau
Art Deco Needlework Carpet
c. 1930; 4.27 x 3.33m (14ft x 10ft 11in)
New York, $85,000 (£32,000) 6.VI.96

Boiçeau gained recognition as a carpet designer during the 1920s
in Paris. His skilful use of colour was combined with a knowledge
of 19th-century weaving techniques. The carpets were executed in
a tight, flat weave resembling the finest tapestries of the 18th century,
but the interrelationship of colour and form was boldly modern.
He also created luxurious furniture that provided a perfect foil
for his intense carpets. This rug was made for a Chicago apartment,
where it remained from 1929 until 1970.

PRECIOUS OBJECTS

Jewellery

**Ruby and Diamond Pendant-Necklace
and Matching Earrings**

Harry Winston, signed, whole set weighing
135.46 carats; necklace length, 43.15cm (17in)
New York, $3,302,500 (£2,080,575) 26.x.95

Composed of floral medallions set with
cushion-shaped, Burmese rubies, this
necklace and earrings is a Harry Winston
classic. Burmese rubies, considered by
connoisseurs to be the most beautiful in
the world, are extremely rare in large sizes
and have become increasingly hard to find.
The beautiful design of these pieces
combined with the gems' rarity, make them
one of the most important Winston pieces
ever to be offered at auction.

**Emerald and Diamond Necklace
and Earrings**

Fitted box stamped, *'London & Ryder'*
c. 1830; necklace length, 38cm (15in)
New York, $244,500 (£154,035) 25.x.95

This extraordinary necklace supports 11
extremely fine emeralds weighing a total
of approximately 30.00 carats. Along with
old-mine diamonds, the whole ensemble is
set in an intricate gold filigree and beadwork
border. Emerald is a silicate of beryllium
and owes its colour to small traces of
chromium, the same element that gives rise
to the fine red of Burmese rubies.

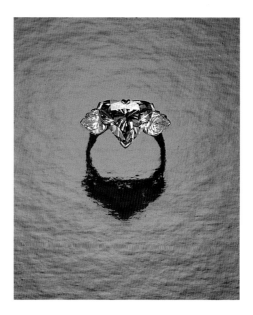

A Fancy Blue Diamond Ring
7.76 carats
Geneva, SF1,763,500 (£953,243; $1,410,800)
16.V.96

This square, step-cut stone is classified as a Fancy Blue. Diamonds come in a wide variety of colours, of which blue is amongst the rarest and most desirable. Historically, most coloured diamonds were mined in India and collected by royalty. These mines were depleted by the end of the 18th century, and after 1900 South Africa became the primary source for fine fancy-coloured diamonds.

Emerald and Diamond Ring
Emerald, 8.02 carats
Geneva, SF751,500 (£406,216; $601,200)
16.V.96

Extremely rare and highly important, this emerald and diamond ring is set with a superb square, step-cut emerald flanked by triangular-shaped diamonds and mounted in platinum. Colombian in origin, the gem possesses a high degree of transparency. Emeralds have undoubtedly been highly valued for thousands of years and, historically, Colombian emeralds have always been the world's finest.

Fancy Deep Blue Diamond Ring
6.70 carats
New York, $3,522,500 (£2,219,175)
25.X.95

The fancy deep blue diamond is flanked by two pear-shaped diamonds and mounted in platinum. Natural fancy blue diamonds derive their colour from boron, making them electrically conductive.

Sapphire and Diamond Pendant on a Diamond Necklace
Pendant signed 'Harry Winston', c. 1960
Sapphire pendant, 150.47 carats;
necklace length, 42cm (16½in)
Geneva, SF3,413,500 (£1,928,531; $3,020,796)
16.XI.95

The octagonal, step-cut Burmese sapphire featured in this magnificent necklace weighs an astonishing 150.47 carats. The sapphire sits within an open framework of pear-shaped and brilliant-cut diamonds. This unusual pendant is illustrated in Laurence Krashe's volume, *Harry Winston: The Ultimate Jeweler*.

Fancy Greyish Blue Diamond Ring
David Webb, signed; 19.45 carats
New York, $3,302,500 (£2,080,575) 26.X.95

This pear-shaped diamond is flanked by half-moon-shaped diamonds and mounted in platinum. The stone is Fancy Greyish Blue and potentially flawless.

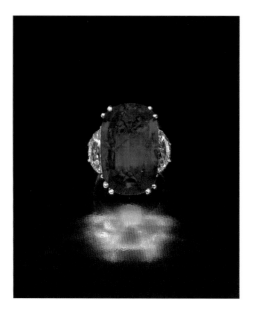

Ruby and Diamond Ring
24.33 carats
Geneva, SF993,500 (£537,027; $794,800)
16.V.96

Of Thai (Siamese) origin, this impressive, cushion-shaped ruby is framed by half-moon-shaped diamond shoulders and mounted in 18-carat gold. The small, circular-cut diamonds of the gallery have a pink tint which enhances the ruby's wonderful, deep colour.

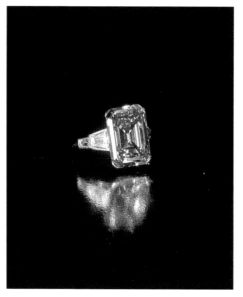

A Fancy Intense Purplish Pink Diamond Ring
Cartier, c. 1925; 7.37 carats
Geneva, SF6,823,500 (£3,855,085; $6,038,496)
16.XI.95

One of the finest pink diamonds to have appeared at auction for many years, this claw-set diamond is particularly notable for the purity of hue and the strength of saturation which impart its truly outstanding colour. It achieved the highest price paid per carat for a pink diamond at auction.

A Diamond Ring
38.88 carats
Geneva, SF1,873,500 (£1,058,475; $1,657,965)
16.XI.95

This highly important ring is claw-set with a step-cut diamond of rectangular shape and cut corners flanked by two tapered baguette stones. The claw setting holds the faceted diamond above the ring so that light can enter and illuminate it.

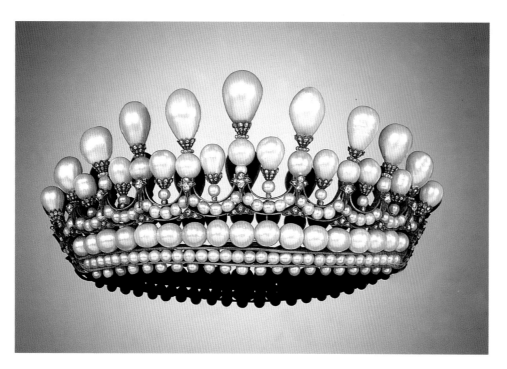

Pearl and Diamond Tiara
Early 19th century
London, £59,800 ($90,896) 28.III.96

According to tradition, this fine tiara was formerly in the collection of Empress Josephine Bonaparte. Certainly, Josephine's passion for jewels is well documented and even after her divorce from Napoleon, when she relinquished the use of the Crown Jewels, she maintained a considerable personal collection. Upon her death in May 1814 an inventory was made detailing over 130 items. The collection was estimated at FF1,923,263, a figure considered to reflect possibly half its true value.

The Lesotho III Diamond
Harry Winston, signed
New York, $2,587,500 (£1,707,750) 24.IV.96
From the Estate of Jacqueline Kennedy Onassis

This marquise-shaped diamond was one
of 18 gems cleaved from the famous rough
diamond that was discovered in Lesotho,
South Africa, in May of 1967 and later
exhibited at the Smithsonian Institution and
the New York Museum of Natural History.
This stone weighs 40.42 carats and was
the third in size to be cut from the rough.
The ring was an engagement present to
Jacqueline Kennedy from Aristotle Onassis.

Pear-Shaped Diamond
38.61 carats
New York, $2,862,500 (£1,774,750)
18.IV.96

Cut in a traditional pear shape, this magnificent diamond is internally flawless.

Unmounted Coloured Diamond
25.85 carats
Geneva, SF2,863,500 (£1,547,837; $2,290,800)
16.V.96

An emerald-cut stone of light blue colour,
this diamond is internally flawless. Coloured
diamonds were introduced to the courts
of Europe in the 17th century by the jeweller
to the court of Louis XIV, Jean-Baptiste
Tavernier, who discovered them on his travels
to India.

Diamond Bracelet
Harry Winston; length, 18.5cm (7¼in)
St Moritz, SF542,500 (£296,448; $459,746)
22.II.96

Designed by Harry Winston, this diamond
bracelet, consists of a triple row of claw-set
diamonds mounted in platinum and set
in a flexible ribbon. Winston (1896–1978)
was the world's largest individual dealer in
diamonds. He was also a cutter of diamonds
and a designer of splendid jewellery set
with precious stones, of which this piece
is a fine example.

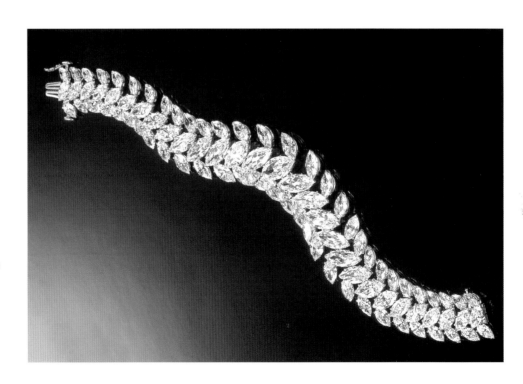

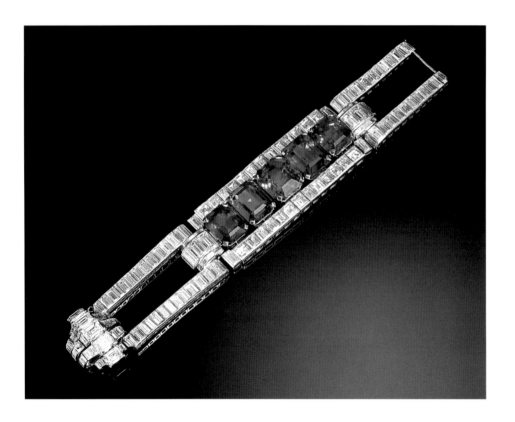

Sapphire and Diamond Bracelet

Van Cleef & Arpels, Paris, signed, *c.* 1935
Emerald-cut sapphires, 78.91 carats;
square-cut baguette diamonds, 43.00 carats
Length, 16.8cm (6⅝in)
New York, $717,500 (£444,850) 18.iv.96

The elegant design of this bracelet typifies
the trend in the 1930s for bracelets that made
a strong fashion statement. Bracelets with
wide straps such as this one appeared on
the wrists of society women and film stars
alike, and were often designed by the famous
Parisian houses of Van Cleef & Arpels and
Cartier. This piece features five sapphires
of vivid blue, perfectly matched and of exceptional quality, within a border of baguette
diamonds.

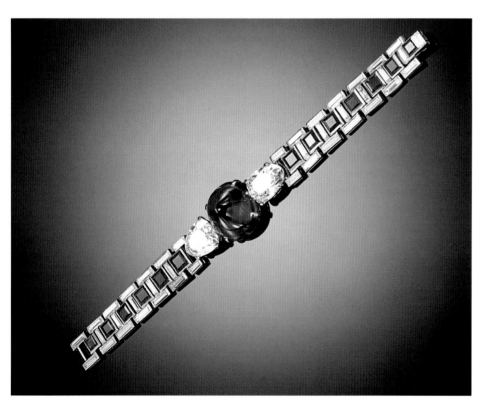

Art Deco Sapphire and Diamond Bracelet

Cartier, *c.* 1930; sapphire, 17.76 carats
New York, $772,500 (£486,675) 26.x.95
Property from the Estate of Mary K. Monell

This wonderful example of Art Deco work
by Cartier is decorated in the centre by
a sugarloaf cabochon sapphire. The A.G.L.
report states that it is of Burmese origin.
The square-cut sapphires and baguette
diamonds of the strap lend it the geometric,
machine-like lines of the Art Deco period
and evoke the modern theme of the 1930s.

Diamond Necklace

Circa 1935; necklace length, 38cm (15in)
Geneva, sf465,500 (£251,621; $372,400) 16.v.96

The front of this necklace is designed as three
garlands of baguette diamonds supporting
brilliant-cut diamonds that are graduated
in size. The sides are accented with baguette-
diamond buckle links. The back segment of
the piece is detachable.

Diamond Necklace
Cartier, signed, *c.* 1960; whole necklace
133.46 carats; length, 37.44cm (14¾in)
New York, $1,377,500 (£867,825) 26.x.95

Using the basic design of the popular *rivière*, a necklace designed with diamonds graduating in size from the centre, individually set in collets or prongs, Cartier introduced some of the more modern elements of Art Deco. This necklace, made in the 1960s, merges these two styles, using square-cut diamonds to alternate with the larger, round stones.

Diamond Necklace and a Pair of Matching Earclips

Harry Winston, necklace signed, 120 carats
necklace length, 38.5cm (15in)
Hong Kong, HK$4,420,000 (£362,295;
$571,650) 21.IX.95

This necklace set with pear- and marquise-shaped diamonds was designed by Harry Winston as a row of stylized floral and foliate motifs. The necklace divides into four segments and can be worn as a bracelet. Set in platinum, which enhances their natural brilliance, the diamonds weigh a total of 120 carats.

Gold, Carved Coral and Diamond Horse Bracelet

Van Cleef & Arpels, France, signed
Length, 21.6cm (8½ in)
New York, $123,500 (£81,510) 24.IV.96
From the Estate of Jacqueline Kennedy Onassis

An avid horsewoman, Mrs Onassis collected many pieces that reflected her love of riding. Designed as a horse's head with cabochon emerald eyes and diamond-studded gold mane, the bracelet combines circular links of carved coral with 18-carat gold and a total diamond weight of approximately 8.00 carats.

A Habille Cameo

Morelli, signed, early 19th century
London, £45,500 ($69,160) 28.III.96

Nicoló Morelli (1771–1830) was a well-known Roman gem engraver patronized by Napoleon I, and this cameo depicts the victorious emperor himself. It is understood that Napoleon made a gift of this jewel to a British friend, who, on hearing of Napoleon's complaint of a lack of books, packed up his entire library in Delhi and sent it to St Helena. Although the ship was lost, the emperor was touched by the man's generosity.

Miniatures & Vertu

**A Two-colour Gold and Hardstone Boite
à Miniatures**
Maker's mark of Pierre-François Drais, charge
and discharge marks of Jean-Baptiste Fouache,
Paris, 1774
Width, 8cm (3⅕in)
Geneva, sf179,500 (£100,279; $158,849) 15.XI.95

This orange agate box with classical motifs features gold
cagework mounts that incorporate the characteristic
branch-hung thumbpiece. It is chased with lemon-gold
laurel leaf-tips and pilasters. The miniatures are painted
en grisaille by J. J. de Gault on a matching orange ground
to resemble cameos. On the lid, a scene of the education
of Bacchus is flanked by two profile medallions. On the
sides and base are further depictions of Bacchic revelry.

**Mrs Cam of Newport, Berkeley,
Gloucestershire**
Isaac Oliver, *c.* 1610
Oval, 5.4cm (2⅛in)
London, £41,400 ($64,584) 6.VI.96

This is an extremely fine portrait miniature by Isaac
Oliver (d. 1617), one of the great protagonists of the art.
Of Huguenot extraction, Oliver was apprenticed to
Nicholas Hilliard, under whose influence he absorbed
the native English tradition. He went on to evolve an
individual style that blended the hieratic linear features
of the English school with a subtle modulation of form
that reflected his awareness and absorption of the
Continental style.

**A Large Russian Silver-gilt
and Shaded Enamel Rooster-Form Kovsh**

Maria Semyonova, Moscow, *c.* 1910
Length, 37.5cm (14¾in)
New York, $23,000 (£14,950) 12.VI.96

The *kovsh*, a Russian vessel used for ladling out drinks, was usually made of silver or hard-wood. This highly decorative example is of silver-gilt enamel with colourfully plumed birds inhabiting flowering, scrolling foliage. A cartouche of flowers on a pink ground is bordered by blue scalework, and the rim is mounted with brightly coloured hardstone cabochons. The prow is in the form of a rooster head, with eyes of red stones, and the handle is drawn up into a wide, flat-shaped tail.

Clocks & Watches

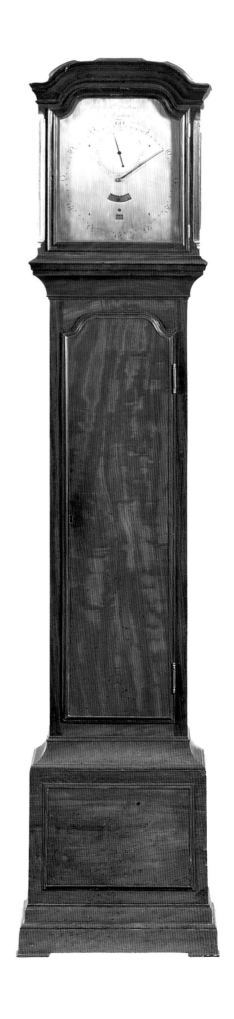

Thomas Tompion, No. 300, *c.* 1700
**An Ormolu Mounted Ebony Grande Sonnerie
and Quarter Repeating Table Clock**
Height, 44.5cm (17½in)
London, £287,500 ($439,875) 14.XII.95

Grande sonnerie table clocks from this early period are extremely
rare, as clocks of such complexity were only attempted by
the foremost makers. It would appear that Tompion made fewer
than 20 *grande sonnerie* spring clocks. This particular example bears
the cypher of Henri-Jules de Bourbon (1643–1709), fifth Prince
de Condé, who was the first owner of the clock.

Matthew Dutton, *c.* 1780
A Small Month-Going Mahogany Longcase Regulator
Height, 197cm (77¾in)
London, £73,000 ($111,690) 7.III.96

This fine example of a longcase regulator has a solid mahogany case
with ogee-arched moulded cornice, panelled top and fluted canted
hood corners. It is signed by Matthew Dutton, who worked in Fleet
Street and was apprenticed in 1771. He was Free of the Clockmakers'
Company from 1779. His father, William, was a partner of Thomas
Mudge and succeeded him in the same year. In 1800 Mathew Dutton
became Master of the Clockmakers' Company, holding the position
until 1825.

John Roger Arnold, Invt. & Fecit, No. 1869, 1802
A Silver Pocket Chronometer
Diameter, 6.3cm (2½in)
New York, $26,750 (£16,853) 21.II.96

Jacob Baumen, No. 3, *c.* 1770
**A Repoussé Silver Quarter-Striking
Alarm Calendar Chaise Watch**
Diameter, 10.5cm (4⅐in)
London, £17,250 ($27,255) 28.IX.95

This chronometer was formerly owned by Cecil Clutton who noted
in *Collector's Collection* that it was 'of the highest quality, fully equal
of anything executed in the life-time of [his father] John'.

The back of this watch, on which two-colour gold masks the
figures and flowers of a *repoussé* classical scene, is highly unusual.
Bigger than pocket watches, chaise watches were travellers'
timepieces, originally designed to hang up in the coach during
the journey.

A. Lange & Söhne, Glashütte, No. 42009, 1901
**A Gold Hunting Cased Minute Repeating Watch
with Chronograph and Register**
Diameter, 5.8cm (2¼in)
Geneva SF71,300 (£39,832; $63,097) 14.XI.95

This is one of 55 Minute Repeaters with Chronograph produced by
Lange & Söhne. Lange was born in Dresden, the son of a gunmaker.
An extremely versatile clock and watchmaker, he constructed astro-
nomical clocks and complicated watches using his ingenious tools
for cutting wheels and pinions. The Glashütte Horological School,
which was initiated by him, did not open until 1878, two years after
his death.

Breguet, No. 3112, 1817
**A Gold Centre Seconds Ruby Cylinder Watch,
Marking Whole Seconds**
Diameter, 5.5cm (2⅕in)
London, £78,500 ($120,105) 14.XII.95

The Frenchman Abraham Louis Breguet was one of the most celebrated watchmakers of the late 18th century and early 19th century.
Not only did he invent new escapements including the Tourbillon,
but the extreme elegance and fine worksmanship of his dials, cases
and movements were far in advance of anything hitherto produced
and even today his designs have rarely been surpassed.

Vacheron & Constantin, No. 355730, c. 1940
**A Gold Minute Repeating Wristwatch
with Subsidiary Seconds**
Diameter, 3.5cm (1⅓in)
Geneva, SF179,500 (£100,279; $158,850) 14.XI.95

The Swiss firm of Vacheron was established by Jean-Marc Vacheron
in 1755. It was his personal ambition to make pocket watches that
would stand out for their quality and elegance. His grandson Jacques
teamed up with a rich friend, François Constantin, in 1891.
By the 1940s, when this watch was made, the company was producing
technically advanced and beautiful watches of simple, classic design.

Patek Philippe & Co., No. 868344, *c.* 1955
A Gold Perpetual Calendar Chronograph Wristwatch
Diameter, 3.8cm (1½in)
New York, $162,000 (£102,060) 30.x.95

This wristwatch with tachometer has three subsidiary dials indicating constant seconds, register for 30 minutes and moon phases combined with the date. Patek Phillipe are renowned for their technical achievements and are credited with having created the world's most complicated watches.

Patek Philippe & Co., No. 861499, *c.* 1950
Gold Minute Repeating Wristwatch
Diameter, 3.3cm (1⅓in)
New York, $277,500 (£174,825) 30.x.95

Production of minute repeating wristwatches seems to have begun sometime in the early 20th century and continued until 1942, when, according to Patek Philippe, the last movement was finished. Minute repeating wristwatches produced in the 1950s continued to use the movements that were made in the previous decade. Although production spanned a period of nearly 50 years, very few examples are known.

Patek Philippe & Co., No. 869432, *c.* 1981
A Pink Gold Sweep Seconds Perpetual Calendar Wristwatch with Moon Phases
Diameter, 3.7cm (1½in)
New York, $222,500 (£140,175) 30.x.95

This wristwatch by the renowned firm of Patek Philippe features a subsidiary dial showing combined date and moon phases. From its inception in 1839, Patek Philippe has produced exquisitely decorated watches. Its principles of manufacturing, whereby every single part of the watch is finished by hand, have not changed over its 150-year history.

Silver

A Set of Seven Queen Anne Silver Casters
Joseph Ward, London, 1705
Heights, one at 24.3cm (9½in),
two at 18.4cm (7¼in), four at 11cm (4¼in)
London, £58,700 ($89,224) 14.III.96

This set, made by Joseph Ward, appears
to be the only set of seven Queen Anne silver
casters in three sizes recorded. The arms
are those of Howe for Sir James Howe,
2nd Baronet (1670–1736) of Cold Barwick,
Wiltshire. The elaborate engraved cartouches
enclosing the armorials have drapery
mantlings and tiered platform bases in the
manner of Blaise Gentot, who is acknowl-
edged as the finest engraver on silver in
England in the late 17th century.

**A Pair of American Silver
Nine-light Candelabra**
Tiffany & Co., New York, 1884
Height, 40.6 cm (16in)
New York, $123,500 (£80,275) 20.VI.96
*From the Jerome Rapoport Collection
of American Aesthetic Silver*

These candelabra are listed in the Tiffany
pattern book as '*Candelabra, Seahorse, Rich*',
and are the only pair made in this pattern.
The stem of one is cast with mermaids riding
dolphins, the other with mermen leading
seahorses, all surrounded by shells and
seaweed. They were completed in the summer
of 1884, using 121 ounces of silver for each
candelabra and had a making charge
of $750.00.

A Pair of Regency Silver-gilt Salvers-on-Foot

Paul Storr, London, 1810

Engraving attributed to Walter Jackson; fully marked
and stamped 'RUNDELL BRIDGE ET RUNDELL
AURIFICES REGIS ET PRINCIPIS WALLIAE LONDINI'

Diameter, 30.5cm (12in); height, 14.6cm (5¾in)

New York, $239,000 (£152,960) 17.x.95

Property from the Meech Collection of Silver, Part Two

Paul Storr was the leading silversmith of the English Regency
period and is known to have worked in partnership with the firm
of Rundell, Bridge & Rundell, for whom Walter Jackson was chief
engraver. The salvers bear the arms of Monson and it is possible
that they were produced by Storr for John George, 4th Baron
Monson (1785–1809) and delivered after his death, or that they
were a christening present for Frederick John, 5th Baron of Monson,
who was born 3 February 1809.

A German Parcel-gilt Silver Nef

Tobias Wolf, Nuremberg, *c.* 1620

Underside inked '*191 Guss II66*', marked on body and foot

Height, 38cm (15in)

Geneva, SF69,000 (£38,547; $61,061) 13.v.96

Nefs, vessels shaped like ships, were used in the latter part of the
Middle Ages to hold the lord's napkin, knife and spoon. By the 16th
century they were mainly table ornaments, or used as the great salt,
and some, like this example, are elaborately detailed. This striking
piece includes a base embossed with sea monsters amongst waves,
as well as billowing sails, rigging and seven figures on board.

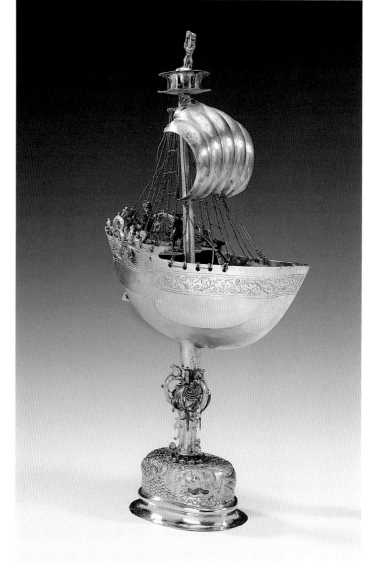

A German Silver-gilt Model of a Ram
Leonhard Umbach, Augsburg, *c.* 1590
Length, 22.5cm (8⅘in)
Geneva, sf111,300 (£62,179; $98,495) 13.xi.95

Formerly in the collection of Baron Heinrich
Thyssen-Bornemisza (1875–1947), this piece
was made by the silversmith Leonhard
Umbach, who was working in Augsburg
between 1579 and 1593 and was the maker
of a fine silver-gilt model of a bear in the
Württembergisches Landesmuseum,
Stuttgart. From the late 16th century, table
ornaments only notionally intended as
drinking vessels were made. Naturalistic
forms included various animals and birds,
although models of rams are rare.

A German Silver-gilt-mounted Tortoise
Maker's Mark MB conjoined, probably
for Melchior Bair, Augsburg, *c.* 1600
Length, 15.2cm (6in)
New York, $118,000 (£75,520) 19.x.95
Property from the Collection of the Late
Saemy Rosenberg

This piece is modelled in the form of a
complete tortoise shell that is fitted inside
with a drawer. Melchior Bair's workshop
produced a large range of domestic silver,
including cups in the form of apples and
at least one in the form of a pear. The latter
is in the Victoria and Albert Museum,
London.

A George II Silver Soup Tureen
George Wickes, London, 1743
Underside engraved with scratch weight
129=11, length over handles, 42.5cm (16¾in)
London, £36,700 ($55,784) 14.III.96

George Wickes (1698–1761) was amongst
the leading Rococo silversmiths of his time.
He was the founder of Garrards, the firm
who are the present-day Crown Jewellers
and was himself goldsmith to Frederick,
Prince of Wales, for whom this fine tureen,
one of a pair, was made. The contemporary
royal arms are engraved on either side,
and the crest of the Prince of Wales appears
on the domed cover.

A French Parcel-gilt Salt
Pierre Rousseau, Paris, 1628
Height, 8.7cm (3½in)
Geneva, SF152,000 (£84,916; $134,513)
13.XI.95

Salts similar to this piece can be seen in
two paintings by the French artist Sebastian
Stosskoff (1597–1657). This example is
a particularly rare survivor – Paris silver
from the early 17th century seldom reaches
the market. The salt here is one of the earliest
to show a step towards the trencher salt,
following the gradual demise of the great salts
of the medieval period, which were the focus
of much ceremony in dining at table.

The Williams Centrepiece
George II Silver Centrepiece (Surtout)
Edward Feline, London, 1730
Height overall, 40.6cm (16in); length overall,
57cm (22½in); width overall, 48cm (19in)
New York, $508,800 (£261,440) 19.x.95

This is now considered the earliest surviving English centrepiece,
or surtout, of complex form. The aim of such centrepieces was
to create a visually exciting centre for the table and to serve as
a practical device, versatile enough to be used at dinner or supper.
For an intimate supper its combination of functions and equipment
would reduce the need for servants. The Williams Centrepiece is
now in the National Museum of Wales.

MARLENE
Dietrich

COLLECTORS'
SALES

Stamps

China 1914–19, First Peking Printing $2
black and blue centre inverted
Hong Kong, HK$597,500 (£51,112; $77,296) 29.IV.96

From 1914 to 1918 Chinese postage stamps were printed by the
Bureau of Engraving and Printing in Peking. On one sheet of 50
of the $2 value, purchased in the Hankow Post Office, the central
'Hall of Classics' vignette was inverted. Records are incomplete as
to the whereabouts of all 50 stamps and some will have inevitably
been lost during the internal upheavals in China. This was probably
only the second occasion on which a multiple of the variety was
offered for sale by public auction.

China 1956, Views of Peking unissued
'Rays of Sunlight' 8f. Tien An Men
Hong Kong, HK$322,000 (£27,544; $41,655) 29.IV.96

This very rare, exquisitely engraved stamp remained 'unissued'
after it was pointed out that neither a rising nor a setting sun
could possibly appear from this perspective in Tien An Men.
The resulting replacement stamp appears, by contrast, singularly
flat and lifeless. The deeply symbolic subject – the Gate of Heavenly
Peace – the technique of recess-printing and the colour chosen,
all recall the 'Golden Age' of similarly famous rare stamps at the
turn of the century.

Rhodesia 1909, Vertical Pair £1 Arms issue with
'Rhodesia' overprint missing on lower stamp
Johannesburg, R121,000 (£18,330; $27,678) 15.V.96

From 1890, postage stamps inscribed 'British South Africa Company' were
used throughout the territory that in 1895 was to be named Rhodesia in
honour of Cecil John Rhodes. In 1909 they were overprinted 'Rhodesia'.
During the process one sheet did not receive an overprint on the last row.
Thus, six vertical pairs exist where the upper stamp is overprinted but
the adjoining one is not. One of the rarest philatelic varieties of Rhodesia,
this example is from the world famous collection of Dr John Strong FRPSL.

New South Wales 1854, Proof Sheet

London, £2,185 ($3,299) 15.v.96

Perkins, Bacon and Co, printers of the world's first postage stamp, the '1d black', also produced many early stamps for far-flung British Colonies. Among these was New South Wales, Australia, and in connection with the production of postage stamps for the Colony's use in 1868, special trial plates of six impressions were made. Lacking the value tablet and with the lower left corner waxed over so it did not print, these proof sheets are found on a variety of papers and in a breathtaking array of colours.

United States of America 1939, Baseball Centennial
3c plate number block of four on first day cover

New York, $14,950 (£9,867) 24.v.96

The date of 12 June 1939 was a big day in baseball, marked by the opening of the Baseball Hall of Fame in Cooperstown, New York. Mr Joseph A. Berinoto of Guttenberg, New Jersey, received a 'first day cover' with a block of four baseball commemorative stamps. What made it stand out from the tens of thousands of similar covers mailed on that day was that it had been autographed by 11 of the 25 founding inductees, including the legendary Babe Ruth.

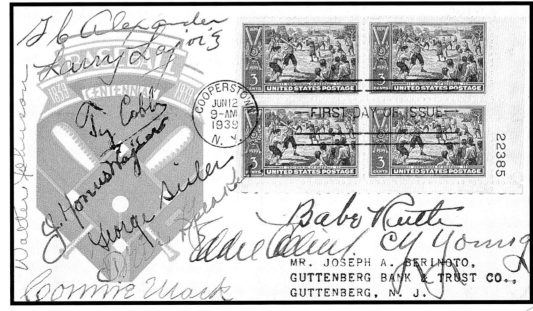

Coins

Roman, aureus of Saturninus, AD *c.* 280
London, £264,000 ($411,840) 8.VII.96

During the third century AD, many Roman generals took advantage of a period of political instability to make their own bids for imperial power. This coin was struck by C. Julius Saturninus, a military commander in Syria, probably as a donative for his troops during his short-lived revolt against the emperor Probus in AD *c.* 280. The rebellion soon collapsed with his murder, and only two coins bearing the name of Saturninus are known, of which this is the only specimen in private hands.

Sicily, doppio trionfo d'oro, *c.* 1479–1503
London, £59,400 ($93,852) 9.X.95

This unique coin was struck under Ferdinand of Spain (1479–1516) prior to the conquest of Naples in 1504, and was probably issued as a presentation piece. It is the earliest known coin of Sicily to feature the monarch's portrait. Ferdinand united the thrones of Castille and Aragon through his marriage to Isabella. In 1492 he expelled the Moors from Granada.

Portugal, justo of D. João II of Portugal *c.* 1489–1495
London, £48,400 ($74,052) 30.V.96

Known in Portugal as 'The Perfect Prince', João II succeeded in strengthening the power of the monarchy by suppressing several revolts of over-mighty subjects. This coin was designed as a symbol of his power and nobility. Issued at Lisbon, it takes its name from the legend stamped on the obverse: '*IVSTVS SICVT PALMA FLOREBIT*' ('The righteous man shall flourish as the palm tree').

Ancient Greek, didrachm attributed to Kalymna, *c.* 500 BC
London £42,900 ($66,924) 8.VII.96

This very rare coin is thought to be from the important Taranto hoard of south Italy, discovered in 1911. Its attribution to Kalymna is based on coins issued there some 200 years later bearing the same designs as well as the name of the island itself. The coin is known to exist at two weight standards, one Greek (as here) and the other Persian, indicating that it might date from the time of the Persian Wars in the early fifth century BC.

USA, quarter eagle, 1839/8-D,
New York, $25,850 (£16,803) 17.VI.96

The mint mark '*D*' on this very rare, exceptionally well-struck coin stands for Dahlonega. This mint in Georgia, which produced only gold coins, was opened in 1838 to accommodate gold miners in the area. On 8 April 1861, the Confederate States seized the mint with $13,345-worth of gold still in its possession. The 1839/8 quarter eagle (2½ dollars) is the earliest issue of this denomination struck at Dahlonega.

Arms & Armour

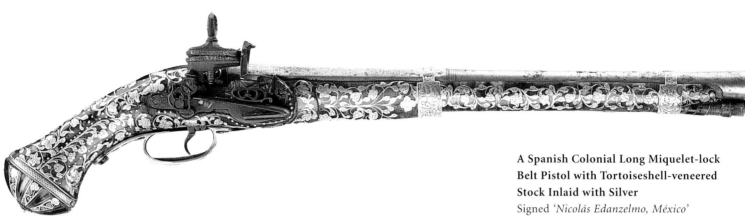

A Spanish Colonial Long Miquelet-lock Belt Pistol with Tortoiseshell-veneered Stock Inlaid with Silver
Signed 'Nicolás Edanzelmo, México'
dated 1692
Sussex, £28,750 ($44,562) 15.VII.96

Currently there are next to no recorded details of a history of gunmaking in the Spanish colonies of Mexico and Cuba that pre-date the first quarter of the 18th century. In this regard the existence of this signed and dated pistol is very significant. The maker was most probably an immigrant from the Catalan town of Ripoll, as the lock exhibits features closely related of those of Ripoll origin.

An Important Spanish Gold-damascened Iron Priming-flask made for the Farnese Family, Dukes of Parma and Piacenza
Late 16th Century
8.6cm (3⅜in)
New York, $20,700 (£13,455) 14.VI.96

An ancient Italian noble family, the Farnese ruled Parma and Piacenza from 1545 to 1731. This flask is likely to have belonged to Duke Alessandro Farnese, one of the greatest generals of the 16th century. He worked in the service of his uncle, Philip II of Spain, and in 1578 was appointed Governor of the Netherlands. In 1590 he led the Spanish army against Henry IV of France. The damascened designs decorating the flask are closely related to those found on Spanish parade shields of the period.

Sporting Guns

Boss & Co.

A Game-Scene-Engraved 12-Bore Selective Single-Trigger Assisted-Opening Sidelock Ejector Gun, No 5210, 1904
Gleneagles, £20,700 ($32,085) 28.VIII.95

Boss & Co. is one of the finest gunmakers in London. The business was founded in 1812 at 73 St James Street. The company mantains a high quality of craftsmanship to this day, operating from its Dover Street premises. This particular gun was probably engraved by Harry Kell who is regarded as the best engraver of this period. His studio was in Soho, where he undertook work for many London gunmakers.

J. Purdey & Sons

A 12-Bore Hammer Ejector Gun, No 15029, 1895
London, £9,200 ($13,939) 1.V.96

This gun was built for Sir Harry Stoner as the No. 1 gun of a pair. Equerry to Queen Mary, Gentleman Usher to Queen Victoria, Edward VII and George V, Sir Harry was one of the finest shots in the country. He appears often in the game cards of that period with HRH The Prince of Wales, Lord de Grey and other notable shots. Due to the advent of the hammerless gun, relatively few hammer ejector guns were built, although some sportsmen believed them to be safer.

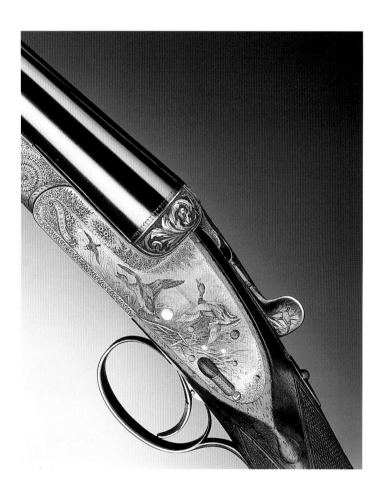

War Medals

A Field Marshal's Baton with G.C.B. and Crimean War Awards: Field Marshal Sir Richard Dacres, Royal Artillery

Sussex, £21,850 ($33,649) 28.XI.95

Sir Richard Dacres was born in 1799, son of Vice-Admiral Sir Richard Dacres G.C.H. He was created Major-General and a Knight Commander of the Bath for his 'distinguished services' in the Crimean War. Further honours followed at the end of the War when he was made a Commander 1st Class of the Military Order of Savoy and a Knight of the 2nd Class of the Turkish Order of Medjidjie. He was promoted within the Order of the Bath to G.C.B. in 1869 and became a Field Marshal in 1886.

The D.S.O. (and two bars) Group to Major-General Orde Wingate, legendary leader of the Chindits

Sussex, £56,500 ($87,010) 11.IV.96

'There was a man of genius who might well have also become a man of destiny', said Winston Churchill of Major-General Wingate following his untimely death in an air crash in northern Assam in March 1944. As the innovative and inspiring leader of Chindit forces in Burma in 1943–4, Wingate holds an assured place in military history. These awards were accompanied by his revolver and uniforms, in addition to his famous 'Wolseley' helmet, which was recovered from the wreckage of his aircraft.

Musical Instruments

A Two-Manual Harpsichord
Andreas Ruckers, Antwerp, 1623
Inscribed '*Andreas Ruckers me fecit Antwerpiæ 1623*'
Length, 2.36m (7ft 11in); width, 94cm (3ft 1in)
London, £89,500 ($141,410) 8.XI.95

The Ruckers family were pre-eminent makers of plucked keyboard
instruments during the 16th and 17th centuries. Their harpsichords
were so admired for their tonal qualities that 18th-century makers
would often update them rather than build their own. This process
usually involved extending the compass, replacing the keyboards
and building more fashionable casework. Examples of Ruckers
harpsichords altered in England, such as this one, are rare. Externally
it resembles the work of one of the great English makers, but the
beautifully decorated soundboard reveals its true origins.

A Violin
Giovanni Francesco Pressenda, Turin, 1832
Labelled '*Joannes Franciscus Pressenda q Raphael
fecit Taurini anno Domini 1832*'
Length of back, 35.6cm (14in)
London, £128,000 ($195,840) 19.III.96

The deep red varnish and understated figure in the wood of the
back of this violin are typical of Pressenda's instruments of 1829–38.
A pioneer of the prestigious Turin School, his contribution to the
evolution of the violin is only now being reflected in the marketplace.
Although born in Piedmont in 1777, Pressenda learnt his craft
in Cremona with Lorenzo Storioni, one of the last makers of the
'Golden Age' of Cremonese luthiers, which included Amati, Guarneri
and, of course, Stradivari.

Vintage & Veteran Cars

1950 Aston Martin Prototype DB2 Drophead Coupé
Birmingham, £54,300 ($81,993) 6.v.96

Formerly owned by David Brown of the Aston Martin company,
whose initials, 'D.B.', were to signify most of the postwar Aston
Martin production, this attractive Drophead Coupé was the
prototype design for the successful DB2 model. Whilst in company
ownership it was exhibited at the London Motor Show in 1950
and featured in the Motor Sport road test a year later. Offered in
original condition, it had resided in the same ownership since 1970.

Wine

1982 Château Mouton Rothschild
One dozen bottles
New York, $5,175 (£3,364) 11.v.96

This is a stellar wine of the super-exotic 1982 vintage in Bordeaux, with all the ripe fruit and flavour one expects from this great First Growth. From the outset, Mouton Rothschild in this vintage showed special qualities, and its price has gradually outstripped other First Growths. The label for this vintage was produced by John Huston, who was a friend of the late Baron Philippe de Rothschild, and a suitably larger-than-life character to match this extraordinary wine.

1985 Domaine de la Romanée-Conti Methuselah Collection
London, £148,500 ($224,235) 15.v.96

One of only half a dozen complete sets made in this excellent Burgundy vintage, this collection included the six great red Grands Crus of the Domaine, as well as the superb white Montrachet. The buyer can now compare the tiny Romanée-Conti with La Tâche, Richebourg with Romanée-St-Vivant, and Grands Echézeaux with Echézeaux. Methuselahs hold six litres of wine, the equivalent of eight bottles, thus the wine will age beautifully and could well be the centre-piece for an historic millennium dinner.

Collectibles

Blonde Venus, 1932
Paramount lithograph, art by R. Vogl,
Austrian, linen backed, near mint condition
2.74 x 1.27m (9ft x 4ft 2in)
New York, $25,300 (£16,445) 7.XII.95

In this poster for Josef von Sternberg's
legendary film *Blonde Venus*, Vogl made
Marlene Dietrich's hips and thighs fuller,
her slip see-through and hid her arms with
gloves and a fur coat. The reference was
to the statue of the *Venus de Milo*. One
of two known existing pre-Code posters,
it is amongst the top three ever designed.

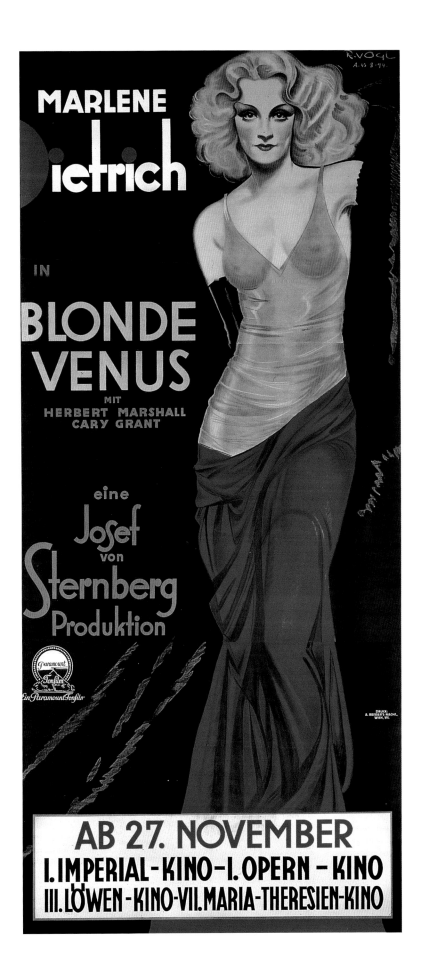

**Pocahontas, Powhatan, John Smith and Indians Pocahontas:
'Loud are the drums of War...'**
49.5 x 63.5cm (19½ x 25in)
New York, $18,400 (£11,960) 24.11.96

Featuring some of the best and most beautiful animation artwork brought to the screen by Walt Disney Studios, *Pocahontas* is a romanticized tale of an American Indian heroine who encounters a British adventurer, Captain John Smith. In this artwork, the image of Pocahontas is superimposed on the cliff where Smith is shortly due to die.

Walt Disney Studio
Pinocchio, 1940
Gouache on trimmed celluloid applied to matching watercolour production background, with production notes at bottom and on back. 30.5 x 40.6cm (12 x 16in)
New York, $120,200 (£78,052) 18.XII.95

This is a key set-up from Disney's famous movie, depicting Geppetto playing with Pinocchio as Figaro echoes his movements. Disney's second animated feature, *Pinocchio* is regarded as one of the best cartoons ever made. Even more sophisticated than Disney's first film, *Snow White and the Seven Dwarfs*, it cost a staggering $2,600,000 to make due to the extensive use of the multi-plane camera.

Action Comics No. 1, June 1938, D.C. Comics
New York, $61,900 (£40,235) 28.VI.96

The first issue of *Action Comics* marked the debut of Jerry Siegel and Joe Shuster's legendary character Superman. It was the most important comic book ever published and, in tandem with Superman, one of the most influential, prevailing for over five decades. This particular copy, in excellent condition, came from the personal collection of a writer of this era and has remained untouched for over 50 years.

Manned Lunar Programme Spacesuit, March 1968: Prototype of pressure suit intended for extra-vehicular activity for the crew of the orbital lunar module
1.6m (5ft 3in)
New York, $34,500 (£22,770) 16.III.96

The Soviet 'Orlan' N1 prototype was a further development of the 'SKV' model of the previous year, with greatly improved mobility at shoulders and knees. This suit was used for on-ground engineering tests, including those made in a low-temperature vacuum chamber. Because it was not needed for the tests, the backpack was left empty of equipment; no self-contained life support system was installed. Instead, a life support of oxygen, ventilation and water was provided from the onboard system through the torso section.

Henri Matisse
Costume for a Mourner in *Le Chant du Rossignol*, 1920
London, £40,000 ($61,200) 14.XII.95
The Diaghilev and Ballets Russes Costumes from Castle Howard

Stravinksy's ballet *Le chant du Rossignol*, based on Hans Christian Andersen's *The Nightingale*, was first performed in Paris in 1920, choreographed by Leonide Massine. The decor and costumes were designed and handpainted by Matisse. This voluminous outfit is of ivory felt applied with midnight blue velvet triangles. The hood incorporates two mule-like ears and a pair of horns painted with black stripes.

Jimi Hendrix's Peacock-Feather Waistcoat, 1967/8
Sold with a colour poster and two 8 x 10in photographs of Hendrix wearing the garment and a letter of provenance
London, £24,150 ($37,674) 14.IX.95

Edged in green with an olive-coloured, crushed-velvet lining and applied with yellow and green sequins, this flamboyant peacock-feather waistcoat was typical of Jimi Hendrix's highly individual taste in clothing. It was worn when the Experience appeared at the Fillmore East, 10 May 1968.

Rare 'Rival' Cast Iron Mechanical Bank

Patented 21 May, 1878 by Daniel James
McLean, manufacturer unknown,
11.1 cm (4⅜in)
New York $54,050 (£22,955) 16.XII.95

This house-form money-bank is in excellent
condition. The brown-painted monkey holds
the coin in his arms and deposits it into the
building through a transom opening above
the doorway. Applied to the roof is a
lithographed scrap of flowers and a hand
presenting a card that reads *'Call me Thine'*.

A Fine Märklin 'Volta' Painted
Tinplate Paddle-Steamer

German, *c.* 1909
58cm (22¾in)
London £27,600 ($41,676) 23.V.96

A clockwork mechanism drives both wheels
of this highly detailed tinplate paddle-steam-
er. Features include two ventilators, a pair
of lifeboats, funnel, wheel house, hatch, mast
with headlamp, anchor winch, red and white
striped canopy with benches below occupied
by nine passengers, and decks that are handpainted with simulated planking.

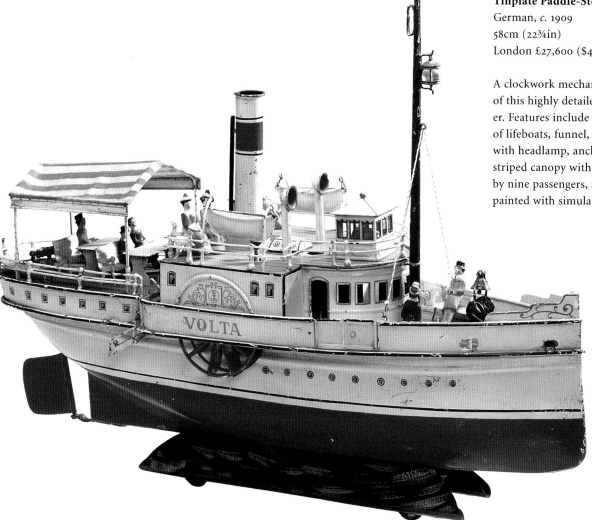

**A Silver Mounted Set of Carved Boxwood Chessmen
in Tortoiseshell veneered Case, Augsburg, *c.* 1735**
With C. B. silvermark for Christian Baur of Augsburg
Board, 41 x 41 x 9cm (16 x 16 x 3½in); kings, 8cm (3⅛in), rooks,
9cm (3½in)
London, £96,100 ($145,111) 23.v.96

These chess pieces either have silver bases and green stained ivory
platforms, or silver-gilt bases with mother-of-pearl platforms.
The ivory-mounted king and queen are carved in elaborate European
regalia, the other pair as native warriors. Gesturing bishops appear
as merchantmen wielding staffs, the knights as dancing youths, the
rooks as elephants laden with castellated turrets bearing a rock hurler
and a staff bearer. Pawns are variously carved as humble, drunken
peasants, or tradespeople with superbly rendered, characterful faces.

A Navy Board Model of a William & Mary Royal Yacht
English, 1689–1694
80.5 x 20.5 x 23cm (31¾ x 8 x 9in)
London, £287,500 ($439,875) 30.v.96
Sold on behalf of John Montagu, 11th Earl of Sandwich

Sold for a record-breaking figure, this early model is the most
important Navy Board example to have appeared at auction for 20
years. It is thought to be a 1:32 scale model of the Royal Yacht *Fubbs*,
built in 1682. 'Fubbs', a 17th-century word meaning 'small chubby
person', was Charles II's nickname for his favourite, the Duchess of
Portsmouth. Navy Board models are amongst the finest ship models
ever made, perfectly reproducing the detail of naval ships and using
the best of materials.

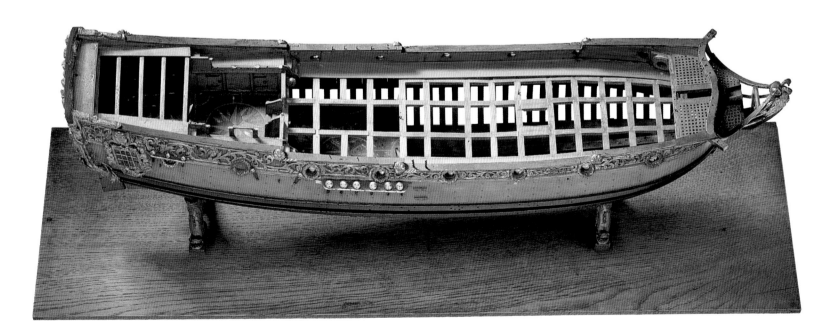

Country House Sales

Hadspen House
Castle Cary, Somerset

In May 1996, Sotheby's sold the selected contents of one of the most handsome houses in Somerset, along with those of three other notable houses in the south-west of England. The Hobhouse family have lived at Hadspen since 1785. Originally cosmopolitan Bristol traders and later influential diplomats and lawyers, they collected an eclectic variety of works of art, including English and Continental furniture, Victorian paintings, and Oriental and European ceramics. Hadspen's beautiful garden, well-known through the work of Penelope Hobhouse, is visited by more than 20,000 people every year.

A Pair of Bronze and Gilt-Bronze Candelabra
French, late 19th century
Height, 1.62m (5ft 4in excluding pedestal)
Somerset, £46,600 ($71,298) 29.v.96

In addition to property from Hadspen, the sale included items from Aynhoe Park and Ilford Manor belonging to Mrs Elizabeth Cartwright-Hignett. Her ancestor Sir Fairfax Cartwright was British Ambassador to Vienna from 1908 to 1913. Obliged to furnish the Embassy, he purchased suites of chairs, torchères, tapestries and Chinese vases suitable for the palatial interiors. These candelabra, each with two figures of putti holding a fluted urn, feature in the series of lavish photographs recording the objects bought for the Embassy.

The East Wing, Ickworth
Surrey

Sotheby's auctioned the contents of the
Marquess of Bristol's private apartments at
his family seat, Ickworth, in June 1996. The
Hervey family, later the Earls and Marquesses
of Bristol, have owned the estate since the
mid-15th century. Built in 1792 and over
700 feet long with a 100 foot central rotunda
modelled on the Pantheon, it is the most
extraordinary of all 18th-century English
houses. This picture shows the Morning
Room, featuring a range of objects sold
at the auction, including van Dyck's *Self
Portrait of the Artist with a Sunflower*.

Studio of Sir Anthony van Dyck
Self Portrait of the Artist with a Sunflower
Inscribed 'A. Van Dike/by Van Dike'
Oil on canvas, in a carved wood frame
58.5 x 72.5cm (23 x 28½in)
Suffolk, £210,500 (324,170) 12.VI.96

The Ickworth sale offered a number of
paintings associated with van Dyck. This
is a studio version of the original in the
Duke of Westminster's collection which was
painted *circa* 1635–6. The chain worn by the
artist was a gift from Charles I acknowledging
him as his 'principal painter'. In art history
the sunflower has been seen as a symbol for
the dependent relationship between subject
and king. Thus the benevolence shown to
van Dyck by the monarch is reflected in
this work.

PRINCIPAL OFFICERS AND SPECIALISTS

Diana D. Brooks
President and
Chief Executive Officer

Simon de Pury
Chairman,
Sotheby's Europe

Henry Wyndham
Chairman,
Sotheby's United Kingdom

John L. Marion
Honorary Chairman,
Sotheby's North America

Richard Oldenburg
Chairman,
Sotheby's North America

Julian Thompson
Chairman,
Sotheby's Asia

George Bailey
Managing Director,
Sotheby's Europe

William F. Ruprecht
Managing Director,
Sotheby's North America

C. Hugh Hildesley
Executive Vice President,
Sotheby's North America

American Decorative Arts
& Furniture
Wendell Garrett
New York (212) 606 7137
Leslie B. Keno
New York (212) 606 7130
William W. Stahl, Jnr
New York (212) 606 7110

American Folk Art
Nancy Druckman
New York (212) 606 7225

American Indian Art
Ellen Napiura Taubman
New York (212) 606 7540

American Paintings,
Drawings & Sculpture
Dara Mitchell
New York (212) 606 7280
Peter B. Rathbone
New York (212) 606 7280

Animation & Comic Art
Jon Baddeley
London (0171) 408 5205
Dana Hawkes
New York (212) 606 7424

Antiquities & Indian Art
Oliver Forge (antiquities)
London (0171) 408 5110
Richard M. Keresey (antiquities)
New York (212) 606 7328
Brendan Lynch (Indian)
London (0171) 408 5154
Carlton Rochell (Indian)
New York (212) 606 7304

Applied Arts from 1850
Barbara E. Deisroth
New York (212) 606 7170
Philippe Garner
London (0171) 408 5138

Arms, Armour & Medals
David Erskine-Hill (medals)
Sussex, 01403 783933
Margaret Schwartz
New York (212) 606 7260

Books & Manuscripts
Paul Needham
New York, (212) 606 7385
David N. Redden
New York (212) 606 7386
Dr Stephen Roe
London (0171) 408 5286

British Paintings 1500–1850
David Moore-Gwyn
London (0171) 408 5406
James Miller
London (0171) 408 5405
Henry Wemyss (watercolours)
London (0171) 408 5409

British Paintings from 1850
Martin Gallon (Victorian)
London (0171) 408 5386
Susannah Pollen (20th c)
London (0171) 408 5388
Simon Taylor (Victorian)
London (0171) 408 5385

Ceramics
Peter Arney
London (0171) 408 5134
Letitia Roberts
New York (212) 606 7180

Chinese Art
Carol Conover
New York (212) 606 7332
Noah Kuperman
New York (212) 606 7334
Colin Mackay
London (0171) 408 5145
Julian Thompson
London (0171) 408 5371

Clocks & Watches
Tina Millar (watches)
London (0171) 408 5328
Daryn Schnipper
New York (212) 606 7162
Michael Turner (clocks)
London (0171) 408 5329

Coins
Tom Eden (ancient & Islamic)
London (0171) 408 5313
James Morton
(English & paper money)
London (0171) 408 5314
Paul Song
New York (212) 606 7391

Collectors' Department
Dana Hawkes
New York (212) 606 7424
Hilary Kay
London (0171) 408 5020

Contemporary Art
Florence de Botton
Paris 33 (1) 42 66 40 60
Elena Geuna
London (0171) 408 5402
Tobias Meyer
London (0171) 408 5400
Robert Monk
New York (212) 606 7254
Leslie Prouty
New York (212) 606 7254

European Works of Art
Margaret Schwartz
New York (212) 606 7250
Elizabeth Wilson
London (0171) 408 5321

English Furniture
& Decorations
Graham Child
London (0171) 408 5347
Larry J. Sirolli
New York (212) 606 7577
William W. Stahl, Jnr
New York (212) 606 7110

French & Continental
Furniture & Decorations
Phillips Hathaway
New York (212) 606 7213
Thierry Millerand
New York (212) 606 7213
Alexandre Pradère
Paris 33 (1) 42 66 40 60
Mario Tavella
London (0171)408 5052

PRINCIPAL OFFICERS AND SPECIALISTS

Garden Statuary
& Architectural Items
James Rylands
Sussex (01403) 783933
London (0171) 408 5073
Elaine Whitmire
New York (212) 606 7285

Glass & Paperweights
Simon Cottle
London (0171) 408 5133
Lauren K. Tarshis
New York (212) 606 7180

Impressionist & Modern Paintings
Alexander Apsis
New York (212) 606 7360
Melanie Clore
London (0171) 408 5394
Philip Hook
London (0171) 408 5223
Andrew Strauss
Paris 33 (1) 4266 4060
Michel Strauss
London (0171) 408 5403
John L. Tancock
New York (212) 606 7360

Islamic Art & Carpets
Professor John Carswell
(works of art)
London (0171) 408 5153
Jacqueline Coulter (carpets)
London (0171) 408 5152
Richard M. Keresey (works of art)
New York (212) 606 7328
Brendan Lynch (works of art)
London (0171) 408 5154
Mary Jo Otsea (carpets)
New York (212) 606 7996

Japanese Art
Neil Davey
London (0171) 408 5141
Ryoichi Iida
New York (212) 606 7338
Suzanne Mitchell
New York (212) 606 7339

Jewellery
David Bennett
Geneva 41 (22) 7 32 85 85
John D. Block
New York (212) 606 7392
Alexandra Rhodes
London (0171) 408 5311

Judaica
David Breuer-Weil
Tel Aviv 972 (3) 22 38 22
Paul Needham (books)
New York (212) 606 7385
Camilla Previté
London (0171) 408 5334
Kevin Tierney (silver)
New York (212) 606 7160

Korean Works of Art
Ryoichi Iida
New York (212) 606 7268

Latin American Art
Isabella Hutchinson
New York (212) 606 7290
August Uribe
New York (212) 606 7290

Musical Instruments
Leah Ramirez
New York (212) 606 7938
Graham Wells
London (0171) 408 5341

19th Century
European Furniture
& Works of Art
Jonathan Meyer
London (0171) 408 5350
Elaine Whitmire
New York (212) 606 7285

19th Century European
Paintings & Drawings
Michael Bing
London (0171) 408 5380
Benjamin Doller
New York (212) 606 7140
Nancy Harrison
New York (212) 606 7140
Rob Mulders
Amsterdam 31 (20) 627 5656
Pascale Pavageau
Paris, 33 (1) 42 66 40 60

Old Master Paintings
& Drawings
Alexander Bell
London (0171) 408 5420
Frédéric Gourd
Paris 33 (1) 42 66 40 60
Gregory Rubinstein (drawings)
London (0171) 408 5417
Scott Schaefer (drawings)
New York (212) 606 7222
Julien Stock
Rome 39 (6) 684 1791
George Wachter
New York (212) 606 7230

Oriental Manuscripts
Marcus Fraser
London (0171) 408 5332
Carlton Rochell
New York (212) 606 7304

Photographs
Denise Bethel
New York (212) 606 7240
Philippe Garner
London (0171) 408 5138

Portrait Miniatures
& Objects of Vertu
Heinrich Graf von Spreti
Munich 49 (89) 291 31 51
Gerard Hill
New York (212) 606 7150
Haydn Williams
London (0171) 408 5326

Postage Stamps
Richard Ashton
London (0171) 408 5224
Robert A.G.A. Scott
New York (212) 606 7288

Pre-Columbian Art
Stacy Goodman
New York (212) 606 7330
Fatma Turkkan-Wille
Zürich 41 (1) 422 3045

Prints
Mary Bartow (19th & 20th c)
New York (212) 606 7117
Nancy Bialler (old master)
New York (212) 606 7117

Jonathan Pratt
London (0171) 408 5212
Nina del Rio (contemporary)
New York (212) 606 7113

Russian Paintings
& Icons
Michael Bing
London (0171) 408 5380
Gerard Hill
New York (212) 606 7150

Silver
Harold Charteris (continental)
London (0171) 408 5106
Ian Irving
New York (212) 606 7160
Kobus du Plessis
Paris 33 (1) 4924 9437
Kevin L. Tierney
New York (212) 606 7160
Peter Waldron (English)
London (0171) 408 5104

Sporting Guns
Adrian Weller
Sussex (01403) 783933

Tribal Art
Jean G. Fritts
New York (212) 606 7325

Vintage Cars
Martin Chisholm
London (0171) 408 5320
David Patridge
New York (212) 606 7920

Western Manuscripts
Dr Christopher de Hamel, FSA
London (0171) 408 5330

Wine
Jamie Ritchie
New York (212) 606 7207
Serena Sutcliffe, MW
London (0171) 408 5050

251

Chapter Illustrations

pages 40–41: Hippolyte Bayard, *Still Life Composition with Statue and Bas Reliefs*, early 1850s (enlarged); albumen print from glass negative mounted on card; 33 x 26.8cm (13 x 10½in) London, £28,750 ($42,838) 2.v.96.

pages 120–21: François Marie Arouet de Voltaire, *Zadig ou la destinée*, Art Nouveau style binding by Marius Michel, London, £23,000 ($35,650) 21.XI.95 (see p.127).

pages 140–41: *An Assyrian Gypsum Relief Fragment from Room 1 of the North-west Palace of Assurnasirpal II at Nimrud*, reign of Assurnasir-pal II, 885–856 BC; 78.7 x 90.2cm (31 x 35½in) New York, $5,667,500 (£3,683,875) 8.XII.95. From the Mr and Mrs Klaus G. Perls Collection of Antiquities (see p.167).

pages 206–7:
Above: *A Natural Grey Pearl and Diamond Necklace*, natural pearls in various shades of grey, spaced by diamond rondels; length, 40cm (15¾in) Geneva, SF344,500 (£182,275; $275,600) 16.v.96.
Below left: *One of a Pair of Natural Grey Pearl and Diamond Earclips*, Geneva, SF93,700 (£49,577; $74,960) 16.v.96.
Below right: *A Natural Grey Pearl and Diamond Brooch*, Geneva, SF91,500 (£48,413; $73,200) 16.v.96.

pages 230–31: *Blonde Venus*, 1932, Paramount, lithograph, art by R. Vogl, 2.74 x 1.27m (9ft x 4ft 2in) New York, $25,300 (£16,445) 7.XII.95 (see p.241).

Publisher's Acknowledgments

The publisher would like to thank Ronald Varney, Suzanne McMillan, William F. Ruprecht, Amanda Brookes, Luke Rittner, Lynn Stowell Pearson, Julie Liepold, Annabelle Brown, David Lee and all the Sotheby's departments for their help with this book.

Prices given throughout include the buyer's premium applicable in the saleroom concerned. These prices are shown in the currency in which they were realized. The sterling and dollar equivalent figures, shown in brackets, are based upon the rates of exchange on the day of the sale.

Photographic Acknowledgments

The publisher would like to thank the following photographers and organizations for their kind permission to reproduce the photographs in the book:

22 © Marilyn Silverstone/ MAGNUM; 23, 24 (above), 25, 26 (above) Sasha Gusov/Sotheby's; 24 (below) The John F. Kennedy Library; 28, 29, 31 © Hulton Getty; 30 (above) private collection, (below) The J. Paul Getty Museum; 32 Ken Adlard/Sotheby's; 33 © DACS 1996/private collection; 36 (above) Cecil Beaton Archive/Sotheby's; 194, 213 (above left), 217 (below left) © 1996 by Caroline B. Kennedy, John F. Kennedy, Jr. and the Estate of Jacqueline Kennedy Onassis.

SOTHEBY'S, AMSTERDAM: 159 (right)

SOTHEBY'S, GENEVA: 34, 36 (below), 37, 200, 210, 211 (above centre and above right), 212 (above left, above centre and right), 213 (above right), 215, 218 (left), 222 (above and below), 226 (right), 227 (above), 228 (below)

SOTHEBY'S, HONG KONG: 153 (above and below), 154 (below), 155, 217 (above), 232 (above and centre)

SOTHEBY'S, JOHANNESBURG: 232 (below)

SOTHEBY'S, LONDON: 10–15, 35, 40–41, 45, 48–51, 53–55, 57–59, 61, 62, 64, 69, 72, 76, 77, 84–87, 90, 91, 96–99, 113, 115, 116, 119, 125, 126 (left), 127 (above and below), 128 (above), 129 (below), 130–137, 142, 143 (left and right), 146, 148, 154, (above), 158 (left and right) 159 (left), 168, 169, 172, 175, 177, 179, 181 (above and below), 182, 183 (left), 188, 191, 193 (right), 195, 196, 198, 201, 203 (left), 212 (below), 217 (right), 218 (right), 220 (left and right), 221 (right), 222 (centre), 224, 228 (above), 233 (above), 234 (above left and right, below left and centre), 236 (left and right), 238 (left and right), 239, 240 (right), 245 (above and below), 246 (below), 247 (above and below), 248 (left and right), 249 (above and below)

SOTHEBY'S, MADRID: 44

SOTHEBY'S, MELBOURNE: 111

SOTHEBY'S, MILAN: 92

SOTHEBY'S, MONACO: 190, 192, 203 (right)

SOTHEBY'S, NEW YORK: 16, 18–21, 42, 43, 46, 47, 52, 56, 60, 63, 65–68, 70, 74–5, 78–83, 88–9, 93–95, 100–109, 112, 114, 117, 118, 122–124, 126 (right), 128 (below), 129 (above), 138, 139, 144 (left and right), 145, 147, 149, 150, 152 (above and below), 156, 157, 160 (above and below), 161, 162 (left and right), 163–167, 170, 171 (left), 173, 174, 176, 178, 180, 183 (right), 184, 185, 186 (above and below), 187 (left and right), 189, 193 (left), 194, 197, 199 (above and below), 202 (left and right), 204, 205, 208 (left and right), 209, 211 (above left and below right), 213 (above left and above centre), 214 (above and below), 216, 217 (below left), 219, 221 (left), 223 (left, above and below right), 225, 226 (left), 227 (below), 229, 233 (below), 234 (below right), 235 (below), 240 (left), 241, 242 (above and below), 243, 244, 246 (above)

SOTHEBY'S, SUSSEX: 171 (right), 235 (above), 237 (above and below)

SOTHEBY'S, TAIPEI: 151

SOTHEBY'S, TEL AVIV: 73

SOTHEBY'S, TORONTO: 110

SOTHEBY'S, ZÜRICH: 71